ONE GOLDEN NUGGET

Tech Treats & Treasures

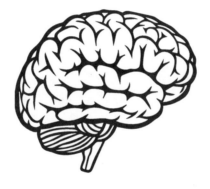

Avril Chester

An award-winning Technology Entrepreneur, experienced
CTO, Author, Podcast Host and Cancer Thriver

Nugget Contributors

Below are the people who contributed to this book and joined us on this amazing nugget journey. Thank you!

Adrian Wakefield	37	Fran Grant	14, 221
Aju Alexander	219	Freddie Quek	99, 131
Alan Walsh	13	Georgina Owens	10
Alison Davis	125	Graeme Hackland	124
Alison McKinna	194, 220	Greg Morley	128
Amanda Khan	100	Ian Wright	189
Ataur-Rahim Ahsan	12, 75	James Endersby	12
Beth Younger	98, 165	Jane Deal	184
Brian Brackenborough	25	Jon Downing	127
Caroline Carruthers	41, 124	Jonathan Wood	38
Catherine Ann Reid	110, 218	Julia Smith	129, 151
Cheryl Cole	220	Katherine Courtney	178
Chris Dadd	38	Kelly Francis	72, 187
Chris Lewis	47	Kim Fitzpatrick	218
Chris Lord	58	Laura Phillips	188
Christelle Heikkila	43, 82	Leon Gauhman	153
Claire Priestley	60	Linda Achan	105, 139
Craig Ambler	188	Mark Chillingworth	27, 207
Daniel Warburton	127, 164	Mark Harrison	84, 162
Danny Attias	36, 53	Mark Lockton-Goddard	87
Darren Sharp	17	Marsha Ramroop	153
Dave Roberts	23, 185	Mathew Mallett	59, 200
Dave Jones	39	Melanie Rose	85
Declan Hunt	48, 126	Michael Long	203
Dominic Hilleard	37, 138	Michelle Spaul	150
Dr Alex Bazin	152	Mignon Mapplebeck	42, 84
Dr Kuldip Sandhu	101, 159	Niel Young	83
Dr. Jacqui Taylor	65, 98	Nigel Hall	192
Eileen Jennings-Brown	29, 99	Peter Job	1, 184
Ezechi Britton MBE	63, 125	Peter Williamson	186

Professor Matthew Cooke	197
Rachel Murphy	45
Reema Gainley	116
Ryan Purvis	115
Sandhya Sharma	13, 59
Sarah Lucas	19, 150
Sean Sadler	83, 172
Serena Walker	100, 135
Shereen Daniels	143
Sherin Mathew	171
Simon Nelson	101
Stephen Johnson	19, 58
Stuart Duthie	36
Su Copeland	113
Tania Ferreira	39, 58
Tiffany Willcox	82, 119
Tiffany Hall	142
Tracey Jessup	50, 151
Trevor Hunt	11, 69
Victoria Russell	219
Vinay Sonchatla	126
Zoe Morris	73

Book & Cover Design - David Torres Mora

Registered office
7-8 Church St, Wimborne BH21 1JH

Published by One Golden Nugget
ISBN: 978-1-4716-6832-6

In memory of and dedicated to Graham Spivey,
celebrating his One Golden Nugget

"Good manners cost nothing
and a smile is priceless"

Contents & chapters

Synopsis	I
Sponsors	III
Purpose	V
Chapter 1 - Life	1
Let's Share Wisdom	9
Chapter 2 - Invent	17
Let's Share Wisdom	35
Chapter 3 - Eat	41
Let's Share Wisdom	57
Chapter 4 - Boost	63
Let's Share Wisdom	81
Chapter 5 - Change	87
Let's Share Wisdom	97
Chapter 6 - Thrive	105
Let's Share Wisdom	123

Chapter 7 - Inclusion   131

Let's Share Wisdom   149

Chapter 8 - Learn   159

Let's Share Wisdom   183

Chapter 9 - Search   191

Chapter 10 - Hope   207

Let's Share Wisdom   217

Synopsis

Start with 200ml of Steven Foster, Founder of One Golden Nugget.

Add a pinch of Avril Chester, Founder of Cancer Central.

Mix with 80+ remarkable Leaders.

When sizzling, add a sprinkle of sponsorship from Intergence and embracent.

Stir in finely chopped 70+ golden nuggets of advice and inspiration.

Add 40g+ of technology stories and a dash of poetry.

Serve 'Tech Treats & Treasures'.

Enjoy a feel-good book full of fun, technology tales and words of encouragement.

Tag your favourite golden nuggets, giggle over a glass of ideas and feel full of motivation.

Relax knowing several tbsps. of your purchase has been donated to Cancer Central, helping people affected by cancer to find the support and information they need.

Sponsored by

Purpose

Avril - Where do I start? When you've been through something life changing, whatever it is, something that really rips up not only the flow of your life but makes you question its purpose, well, what next?

On this occasion, we went through something together, a small thing called a pandemic. We went through it not just as friends or family or neighbourhood, but as a nation and the entire globe. The last few years will be etched into our lives forever, although I'm not actually sure what will be etched in mine. I became a workaholic hermit, with evening tipples, biscuit treats and square-eyed through box sets. Physical contact became hugging my childhood teddy bear, who'd have thought?

But as we take that breath and look on to the future with either excitement, nerves, or relief, I hope this book full of precious nuggets accompanies you wherever you are. On that sun lounger - ooh, remember those? On the train finding a pick me up. On an evening to uncover ideas. On the you know who (yes, I know some of you do), for a giggle or just a light read. This book is meant to be picked up, put down, picked up again, marked, highlighted, tagged with a few of those cute tiny arrow Post-it Notes so you can easily find that golden nugget again. This book is about technology, its leaders, its impact on our lives; stories I'm hoping you've not yet heard and some fabulous golden nuggets and quotes to get you thinking and inspired.

One golden nugget.

Who exactly is behind this inspirational network of sharing and new series of books to tickle your minds? Who encouraged me to write and collate stories from across the world of technology? Who is ultimately responsible for this incredible generosity where the proceeds of your purchase kindly go to Cancer Central so that we can continue to keep the site free from advertising and messaging charges?

Drrrrrrrrrrrrum roll, please. Introducing the formidable and incredible Mr Steven Foster. Or, as I hand over to Steven to share his story, he asks…

Please call me Mr Barlow.

Steven - I've spent just over 30 years of my life trying to build my dream. Each time I thought I was getting there it ended in pieces with me face down in the mud and life stamping on my head. And every time that happened, I somehow find the courage and energy to get up and keep going. I've no idea how. Looking back, anyone with half a brain would say: 'Clearly, this entrepreneurial journey isn't for you, Steven. Go and get a proper job.'

But I never have done. Somehow, I always believe in myself enough to hold onto the image of my success.

When, during my mid-40s, it all crumbled away again I thought it might be time to ask people for help. Please, tell me one thing I can improve. Tell me how you've built that business. Tell me, have you ever had tough moments; or is it just me?

The answers I found were profound. Of course, everyone had been through their own unique challenges. It wasn't just me; it was something every single person had experienced. And some had dealt with far worse than me.

So that's how One Golden Nugget came to be – me asking a few people for a piece of wisdom I could perhaps incorporate into my own mindset and improve. I'd turned my mess into a message.

On that journey, and I don't remember how I originally connected with her, Avril Chester arrived. I believe the people we meet are never there by accident, they come to teach us lessons, show us who we are and bring beautiful life learnings.

Avril had just won an Entrepreneur of the Year award for her work at Cancer Central and I thought she'd have an interesting Nugget to share having been through that very personal experience of cancer and from it looked and found a huge positive. That was to help others. I love that.

She said yes, and her Nugget, 'Stop comparing', changed my life. I realised I'd spent most of my life comparing myself to others, especially Gary Barlow from UK pop band Take That. I'm a songwriter and I was in a boy band in my 20s (without success though), but he had built a life I wanted. He had the success, the fame, the money – all of which, somehow, despite my efforts, had eluded me.

But hold on – 'Stop comparing,' says Avril. Gary Barlow doesn't have my beautiful kids, he doesn't have my mum, or the other people I love. And he hasn't messed up so many times or been broke enough to then invent One Golden Nugget and change people's lives.

The point is, Avril's Nugget shifted me; it made me think. You shouldn't compare yourself to anyone. You are beautiful, unique, and should be grateful for that.

Avril changed my life.

Following up, I asked her to become a Founder at One Golden Nugget, she agreed and then together we formed the idea of creating this book – ask some people in tech about their story, share a piece of wisdom, raise some cash for Cancer Central and in some way change the lives of the people who read the book.

You see, all the mess I've made in my life really has turned into a message – Nuggets change lives! I'm blessed you decided to read this book, thank you.

Steven, Founder One Golden Nugget

Avril - HUGE thank you Steven, I honestly cannot remember how we met either, but I do remember rushing out to St. James' Park to quickly video my golden nugget. So much so, the first few times were dismal, then people kept walking behind – seriously, could they not see I was in the throws of trying out my acting skills? It's embarrassing enough recording yourself let alone attempting it in public. But somehow I got through and that pang of embarrassment pales into insignificance having read your kind words Steven.

As a confession my nugget has grown from something someone else said to me. Someone incredibly impactful in my life, my breast cancer nurse. After diagnosis probably the only words I remember was, 'Don't compare'. Every cancer, every diagnosis, everyone's reactions and everyone's journey is different. 'Don't compare'.

I then played this forward into life, I could see myself comparing in meetings; man she nailed that presentation, wish I could do that. Or wow, look at the impact of what they've built, I can't seem to grow or scale my start-up, what am I doing wrong? I'm in awe of parents who continuously juggle everything when some days getting myself out of bed is a feat in itself. 'Don't compare' soon grew into 'Stop comparing'. Your strengths, uniqueness and situation is different to mine. I needed to re-learn how to believe in myself and trust my intuition. Learn how to take risks again in life and live it to the full in the Avril way.

What's your way?

Hi, I'm Avril, your narrator for the book, welcome, welcome. Sit back, relax and let's get started.

Chapter 1
Life

*A precious gift
An unknown duration,
Let's not drift, and
Giggle through navigation.*

Avril Chester

Avril - Life. One short word that sums up our very existence. It's powerful, precious, and full of different experiences and emotions. We therefore had to start this book with Peter Job, CEO of Intergence. Thank you Peter for being one of our sponsors and making this book a reality, I thoroughly enjoyed interviewing you. You see, I know what life means to me, but what I really wanted to explore was what life means to you.

Peter - I'm not a technologist, but I love technology. If you asked me if I could build a Windows PC or talk in depth about a network, I wouldn't know where to start, but I've got people in the organisation to do that.

I didn't start out thinking I was going to be in tech. My degree was in geography and geology, which turned out to be useless to anybody, apart from myself. It just means I spent hours in front of a microscope, and ended up with a weird eye.

Move on 10 or 12 years from finishing my degree and I started my family. We had my daughter Natalie, and then David, and everything was great.

William followed four years later, and we thought that our young family was complete.

He had a normal birth, but about a week after being born he was rushed into hospital with jaundice. However, it was more serious than that. We were lucky to have a locum doctor who'd been practicing out in Africa and she noticed that William had gone a bit blue around the lips and thought we should get him to Great Orman Street, the renowned children's hospital, immediately.

Straightaway you start to think, this is serious and kind of go into shock.

They took him straight into surgery and I remember feeling helpless. We later found out that William's heart was effectively round the wrong way.

That same feeling of helplessness was something I think we all felt during the pandemic with things going wrong around us that we had no control over. But this was many times multiplied.

A month later William was back in hospital for what was at the time pioneering surgery. Seeing my son go through this was incredibly difficult but what happens is you somehow cope with the situation.

The amazing thing is, as human beings, we can go through sometimes the most terrible traumas and tragedies, but in the vast majority of cases we find coping mechanisms. Whether it's friends or family, those are the times when you have to dig deep.

Luckily William came through it, he's 28 now and fit as a fiddle and I'm delighted to say he's just got married in January this year - to an intensive care nurse!

Avril - Huge congratulations to you and your new wife William from all of us, what amazing news. Peter, my heart lifted when you shared William is now fit as a fiddle. Looking back at this life changing event what nugget of advice would you share?

Peter - Two or three actually. I think firstly, we don't realise what a slender thread of life we live on.

It made me appreciate life in general. And actually, that mindset helped me get through the pandemic, because it's all about scale. I think, sometimes we don't realise what other people have been through because we all have our own personal battles - we have to fight in life.

Second, it showed me the resilience of the human spirit to get through really difficult times.

And lastly, I realised I was a lot stronger than I thought I was and that I could cope with a lot more than I thought I could. It's not until you get tested you find out what you are made of.

Avril - For those that know me, I'm a big fan of social impact technology. In my eyes it is much broader than Tech for Good, which brilliantly describes the act of delivering for a charitable purpose. I'm conscious we all have different definitions so, please, this is just my take on it all, but take the amazing charity Tech for Good and add on 'with profit' initiatives and inventions that impact our society. This is about the entire sum, the complete total of marvellousness and brilliant technology impacting us as humans, our planet and so forth. Regardless of company structure, whether donated, funded, earned, delivered by entrepreneurs or intrapreneurs, technology innovation for social improvement. Whether economic, education, health, sustainability, equality, poverty, environmental and more. This is social impact technology and I know Peter is a big fan as well.

Peter - I mentioned earlier about my Nugget of all of us living on a thread and I think the same is true of the environment.

We live in a delicate balance and we have a social responsibility in terms of the environment and the planet.

I entered this crazy 330-mile bike ride in aid of the Ruth Strauss Foundation. We climbed 29,000 feet over four days, which is the same as Everest, we cycled from Kendall to the Cotswolds and we raised nearly half a million pounds for the Foundation.

I've also done work for the British Heart Foundation, which given my son William's condition is important to me.

With technology I think we are just at the beginning. It's an industry that has only really been around a short time.

My kids can't get their heads around the fact that we used to have to go to a phone box and put coins in it to call people. Technology has moved quite a long way. But on the other hand, it's still in the foundational phase where it's trying to find itself. In IT there simply aren't enough women, so I think a lot of work needs to be done in schools. How many other industries would potentially say they aren't going to use half of the talent pool?

My daughter Natalie is in digital marketing. If you go into any big digital marketing organisation, you'll find it's full of women who are extraordinary talented and creative, and actually do the tech as well. What's more, they do it brilliantly. It's almost as though women move towards the creative side rather than the tech.

So, if we could change that, it would solve a massive problem.

Avril - As a female in technology I get asked the question about women in tech a lot and I'm thankful to all of you who, like Peter, champion diversity of thought and characteristics into the profession. For me, we have a PR exercise to do as I would argue technology requires the most diverse skill set of any profession. Take our Cancer Central chatbot Ask Ave for example, this is about engagement and linguistics. In technology we analyse, spot trends, design experiences, plan, learn, connect, build, buy, negotiate, spot opportunities, use analytics and insights, improve customer interaction, reduce complexity of process, problem solve, experiment, and much, much more. The depth and breadth of the skills required across the tech industry is so vast, there are plenty of opportunities out there.

As Mathew Mallett Cancer Central's Non-Executive Director says: "Technology is a wonderful industry because it requires a whole range of skills in the team. It is also fast moving, and you are constantly learning, therefore it is not a traditional profession where the typical career path starts at higher education, through continual exams and CPD. So why ask for a standard background when this industry is full of people who do not reflect that. People join IT from a range of backgrounds, at various stages in their career. They might be interested in insights and data, digital experiences, or wish to explore ways of communication. The more we are open about how fluid this industry is, the more inclusive we will become."

Inclusivity is an essential backbone of social impact technology as well as innovation and experimentation. It is important we learn from across sectors, and I had one of my best days last year with Peter visiting Ken Hill Farm - beautiful day, bit windy, then the heavens opened for a short time. As we ran inside, a tad drowned, laughing, the visit opened my eyes to how differently they were thinking and how they were challenging convention. Peter, please tell us more and how did you get involved at Ken Hill Farm?

Peter - My sister-in-law Jeanette, asked if I would like to come on a farm walk.

Not my usual thing, but I think in life you have to be inquisitive, so I said yes.

In my Geography degree we did quite a lot on farming and the different techniques. The Holy Grail for farming, certainly since the second world war has been about yields.

What they have done at Ken Hill Farm is counterintuitive. They are pioneering regenerative farming.

So, rather than be stuck to a millstone of high yields, using fertilisers and herbicides, they can use natural techniques. As a result the yield has come down but the profitability has gone up.

It has turned this whole model on its head and now they are leading the UK, if not the world, in terms of regenerative farming training.

I'm doing so much work with them at the moment, using data.

Visualising the data correctly means they have a much better way of forecasting when events are going to happen. Using the power of machine learning and AI you can look historically at weather trends and also forecast.

For me this is the future of farming.

Avril - Did you know 72% of the UK is agricultural, is responsible for 10% of UK emissions yet only 0.5% of GDP? I didn't know either until my trip to the Ken Hill Farm. Seeing how data can support natural techniques in the food we eat was amazing. What also got me were the experiments in farming cycles and harvests. It requires patience. A term not exactly associated with technology.

Thank you so much Peter. Life means so much and we've not even scratched the surface. However, we started with family, which leads me nicely onto life's nuggets.

Let's share
wisdom!

"Don't let anyone tell you that career is a choice. It isn't family or career, life or career, anything or a career. Your career is enriched by other experiences, so do it all."

Georgina Owens
Chief Product and Technology Officer

"People often talk about work/life balance but it's more than that. Twenty years ago I was talking about this with my manager and on the back of a napkin he drew me a picture. Imagine a circle with three equal segments - one labelled Work, one labelled Me and one labelled Family. This was to illustrate how to strike a balance, over time, and the impacts of trying to balance your time between the three segments. First off, is Me time – that includes sleep – but also you need to spend time on yourself to develop your interests and passions and skills. Then there's Family time and Work time. You play a balancing act here driven by circumstances. Urgent deadlines or tough business conditions may mean you are increasing your work time and reducing Family time (or sleep time). The birth of a child or bereavement in the family may mean your Family time has to increase. Hence the size of these segments may increase or decrease over time, BUT there is a finite number of hours in the day. So, aim to 'Strike a balance'."

Trevor Hunt
CTO Advisory Behind Every Cloud, connecting your business to the best technology providers

"Don't compartmentalise, be the best you. Take the finest traits of your professional persona, add the magic from your personal life and blend with your family ethos."

James Endersby
Director of Technology

"Be approachable, be humble, be strong, but never let the cookie crumble!"

Ataur-Rahim Ahsan
Co-Founder and Technical Director @ SloopTech Ltd

"Believe in yourself and have those courageous conversations because the awkward is better than the awful."

Alan Walsh
CEO at Amido

"Live your life with integrity and honesty and you'll never regret anything! There will be challenges and frustrations for sure, but no regrets."

Sandhya Sharma
HR and Lecturer, a keen observer of life

"However gloomy life feels, know that the grey clouds will eventually part and make way for the lovely blue sky that's been there all along."

Fran Grant
Executive Search Consultant, recruiting Senior Technology and
Digital Leadership positions. She is also a mum to three young boys
and a published author of five books

Avril - When life gives you lemons, you make lemonade. I absolutely adore this quote initially coined by Elbert Hubbard. Here we are, a new zest for life (interspersed with days of complete exhaustion). Some declare, "I want to make lemonade". Marvellous. What flavour lemonade as there are now a few. Er, don't know. Many know they simply wish to do something or be involved in creating something new. They wish to invent.

Chapter 2
Invent

I have a focus
A great distraction,
Some hocus-pocus
Creates new action.

Avril Chester

Avril - What's the secret to invention? We each have our own ingredient and for most of us we're rocking it without even knowing because we're moving and shaking in new ways all the time. Try not to put pressure on yourself to find it. The joy is in the discovery.

Thinking of doing something new with tech? Here are some great stories and fun pieces of advice to inspire you.

Darren - "Quick everyone, jump in the car. We need to start driving quickly!"
"What's our destination?"
"What do you mean?"
"Who needs to get in the car, and do we need to bring anything? Like a map?"

"Why do we need to know that? Now hurry up, we should have set off yesterday!"

Why do so many people take this approach to business change? Would they do the same for a weekend trip to the seaside? If so, do they ever reach the beach? Did they bring towels? Their children?

Why do so many people rush to build or buy an IT system with often very little idea of what problems it will solve? Why do they choose to ignore what happens after the system is in place?

If you are asked to 'jump in the car' challenge back with:

1. What problems are we trying to solve and can we write them down?
2. What value are we aiming to derive and can we measure it?
3. Is this more important than yesterday's urgent journey?

Yes, it may be painful.

Yes, you may have some difficult conversations.

But the more you do it the easier the conversations will become. You will achieve a better result – and will be happier for it!

Darren Sharp
A CIO with a passion for problem solving, irritating hundreds of people over the years by asking "why"

Avril - Darren, one of the best words in the dictionary is 'why', we should definitely use it more and channel our inner five-year-old.

Technology is so integral to our lives now, I'm sure many will relate to Sarah's story. Digital is about convenience, before you invent what is the need you are addressing?

Sarah - For me, technology really helps out with what we call today 'the mother load'. Take today, I'm working at my home office desk as is my normal now and I get a text from my daughter asking if we can get the ingredients for her GCSE Food Tech lesson - tomorrow! She sent me the recipe, I clicked the link, was able to add everything to my online shopping account and then to book a slot to go and collect it. So instead of running our own version of Supermarket Sweep, we'll just drive down and collect - another job ticked off the list! Now, if tech can solve whatever she makes, which is unlikely to make it home for consumption, then I'm all in! :)

Sarah Lucas
Award winning IT Transformation and Change Leader

Avril - I think my mum thought the same thing when I was younger, Sarah. What happens if we ask our children, nieces or nephews about the future of tech, perhaps they can give us an idea? Stephen did just that.

Stephen - Technology has made a huge difference to me and my life. As a young lad I always wanted to have my own business. I never knew what it would look like, but I just knew I wanted it. Fast forward to when I hit 33 years old and boom! I had one. And it was a technology business. It is still my pride and joy and single-handedly the best job I've had since my milk round when I was a kid.

But what inspired me?

Well, back when I was at university, I wanted a job that would earn me good money – not in a greedy way – but in a way that would provide a comfortable lifestyle. At that point, technology wasn't a passion at all. It was something that hadn't really bothered me. I had had a ZX Spectrum as a kid and loved playing games; the odd programming element (following steps from a magazine), but generally it was a means of entertainment. At university (c1995/6) we got wind of the internet and email. It was a non-event in many ways. It was just fun, and barely registered on the "wow" factor.

But when I got my first job in technology back in 1998, things changed. I was suddenly exposed to the world of technology, across a whole host of large organisations. I have seen the deep impact it has had on some of the biggest companies in the world – working with 100+ year-old catalogue businesses, that then turn into market leaders in digital (no catalogue in sight); working with market leading music companies and seeing them subsequently almost go into extinction by not moving quickly enough into a technology-first business model. It's not the technology here – it's a means to an end in many ways – but the business leaders leveraging it to transform and develop their proposition. And that has been the key learning and inspiration.

I have seen over 20 years' worth of change driven by technological brilliance and many disasters. In that time, huge sums of money have been ploughed into projects to drive real progress with game changing results.

But when I reflect on my experience, it was luck that I got into the industry – it just wasn't a thing when I was a kid, and therefore the passion and understanding came late in the day.

So, I wondered what a 14-year-old boy – my son – thinks of technology now. Well, that is a whole new ball game. I just dropped the question, randomly whilst he was eating a bacon butty, of what the future would look like, and it was fascinating. At the same age, I'd have probably asked what technology was!

His answer: "I reckon in the near future, there will be nanobots in humans and it'll be able to treat things like cancer, without the person knowing. It'll be cool and we'll probably live a lot longer." He then said: "I think what would be brilliant is if it could create a new layer, that sits just below the ozone layer, so that it protects the planet. We can't keep destroying the planet, so I reckon tech could sort that."

I asked him what he feared about technology. He was very quick in his response. "People are spying on us. I know that whatever we do is being watched and that doesn't feel right. It's just weird that people in China are probably listening to this conversation." What added more intrigue to me on this answer was that morning I had just started reading Nineteen Eighty-Four by George Orwell – Big Brother state! My son also said that he feared that we'd develop robots that would naturally take over – his view is that humans have destroyed a lot of species, so it could be the natural order of events.

These were genuine responses over lunch, no prompting, just a dad posing random questions. What impressed me most was the speed at which he answered. No hesitation, and if he'd had more time, I could have had a list of 20 new ideas and 20 more fears. It's not my place to decide or challenge whether they are viable or not. Let's be honest, technology is developing at such a pace that he may well be spot on.

Wind back two hours before lunch and I'd had to nip to my mum's to help her with her online banking. Since Dad died two years ago, she has had to do all the online stuff herself. And she hates it. As I was dropping my daughter off at work straight after, it turned out to be a flying visit, so I rang Mum on the way to get the laptop on so we can just do it as soon as we got there. When we arrived, she was in tears. The laptop was having a "Windows 10 Update" moment and had been whirling for 15 minutes and wasn't ready. She was worried that she'd make her granddaughter late for work. It was horrible to see. A piece of technology, just having a moment, had the power to upset someone.

So, what is the purpose of these mini stories? For me, they show the generational difference, based on our exposure to, experience, and expectations of technology.

I have lived and breathed it for over 20 years and am amazed by what I have seen. I have also seen lots of fads that barely make it past first base. I am aware of what technology can give, but also cautious in backing every horse in the stable. My son has grown up with technology, like most kids these days. It's glued to their hands, it provides access to information that I (as a 14-year-old) could never have dreamt of and is seen as a divisive thing – good and bad comes with its potential. And as for my mum, it's pure fear. It's not that it exists that worries her, it's the fact that her interactions with it are inherently a nervous experience. When it goes well it's luck, but when it fails, it instantly triggers unwanted emotions.

And that is what technology is now and will be for the foreseeable future. It is something that new generations will join at an entry point, that will no doubt accelerate at a pace significantly faster than the previous generations. We have already seen incredible achievements in the last 20 years and we will see even greater achievements in the next 20 years. In a hundred years we can only hope and pray that the advancements help our planet and the lives of everyone. I think we all believe technology has the power to do that and that is what should excite us. We just need to remember to bring everyone on the journey.

Stephen Johnson
CEO ROQ

Avril - Technology indeed has all kinds of power. Films and series love to dramatically share the worst, have you seen Next on Disney+, honestly not one before bed, a bit too close to home. Have you watched or read something scary recently and in need of a feel-good inspirational story on how technology helps in dangerous situations? Dave has the perfect story for that.

Dave - When Avril Chester approached me to share an example of technology having a positive impact within the community, I immediately thought about the successful development and implementation of a digital tool called Fire Flow. The tool is part of the Stantec.io digital suite of solutions and has been developed in partnership with Thames Water and London Fire Brigade.

As a firefighter, the more you know about an emergency situation, the safer you are. Now, for the first time, London Fire Brigade knows the flow and firefighting capacity of every hydrant in the city, allowing it to better tackle blazes thanks to more informed decision making about where to send station appliances, which hydrants to use and the best routing for hoses.

Fire Flow is a digital twin of every building in London, categorising them based on fire flow requirements and local capacity. The tool not only provides fast, accurate data transfer between water suppliers and the fire service, which helps emergency service teams make more informed, safer decisions during incidents, but it is also being embedded into new construction programmes to improve building safety.

The innovative solution is being utilised to support effective design and construction by helping to estimate the size of firefighting storage tanks required in new buildings based on how much capability exists in the water supply network.

Not knowing if there is sufficient capacity to meet building fire flow requirements poses a significant health and safety risk. The Fire Flow solution provides this critical information, reducing the risk and making a real impact to the health, safety and wellbeing of our emergency service teams.

The in-built hydraulic modelling system provides instantaneous modelling of the network to assess the fire flows available for buildings, analysing for single and multiple hydrants running simultaneously. The emergency service teams can select the location of the fire appliance and the system will choose the best hydrants to use to maximise fire flow and determine routes for the fire hoses.

The Fire Flow system also identifies buildings where mitigation measures may be required to improve available fire flows from fire hydrants or where more hydrants need to be installed. It is a fully adaptable system and could become a template for future conveyance of essential information related to fire fighting capability between water suppliers and fire services.

I am extremely proud to be part of an organisation that is using technology in this way to help protect and save lives.

Dave Roberts
Award-winning Tech Leader,
Global IT Director and Non-Executive Director

Avril - I'm all fired up (boom boom tsch!). There is a serious side to the way technology invention has changed our lives and it would be remiss of us not to discuss it. Perhaps, expectation-wise, none more so than in broadcasting, something that Brian shares with us.

Brian - I have always had this nagging doubt about technology. Something in the back of my mind that says it's a bad thing, that before the age of the iPhone life was much simpler, things were as you expected. News happened in the morning over breakfast, or at night just before bed. And that news felt more reliable because it had been researched, double checked, and confirmed, and then at the end of it there was a nice clip about a dog that could windsurf.

The world's changed, and it is very easy to blame technology. "It wasn't like this before the internet," I hear people cry! And they are right, it most certainly wasn't. Messages took forever to get to their destination, and to get a reply. You'd have to write a letter, put it in an envelope, buy a stamp, go to a post box and actually post it! Then wait for the other person to receive it, read it, write a reply, put it in an envelope... you get the idea. If it was overseas, well, who knows? Unless you were rich and could wait up till the right moment to make the call, which you had probably pre-agreed with the other person, in writing beforehand, by writing a letter, putting it in an envelope... The circle of life, right?

So communications are much better now, unless of course you don't want them to be. Stick it on silent, watch a number ring and become a missed call, don't click on that WhatsApp message and leave it on 'delivered', if you 'air' them, then get ready for some attitude, but the choice is still yours.

(email receipts, I mean, who in their right mind... :)?)

There are so many areas that have changed totally due to the advances that have been made in technology, some clearly positive (medicine) and some that people may have strong opinions on (war). I mentioned the news earlier because the internet has changed this in so many ways, and being in broadcasting, I've seen this first hand.

People want the news now, and they want to consume it in any way possible. They expect something that used to take hours, days, or even weeks to be delivered, to happen in minutes, sometimes seconds. The have a reasonable expectation for this to be accurate, and they want there to be a person on the ground, not just reading it in from a device hundreds or even thousands of miles away from the event. They want it to be clear... clear sound, clear picture, professional... Well, that's just not possible without technology.

In my day (God, I'm not even that old), breaking news was reserved for everything but the biggest stories – war, or the death of a member of the Royal Family. Now you can receive updates about anything on your phone, on top of a mountain – the access to information is truly astounding. Yet, have you ever had that moment when, sat in front of a computer, your mind goes blank on what to search for and you resort to the same favourite websites?

By connecting people technologically, we can connect with people emotionally. We can share moments together, the birth of family members around the world, to the plight of others, to help us better understand what we need to do, to bring more hope and happiness to the world. The problem with technology is people. Not what's been created, but how people choose to use it.

Brian Brackenborough
An information security professional
from the broadcasting industry in the UK

Avril - At the time of writing war has just broken out in Ukraine, with scary loss of precious human life and unknown outcomes. I pray for the safety of those affected and I hope this ends soon. The technology community has already come together, thank you Mark for letting me publish your article in this book.

Mark - Business and technology leadership communities, technology service providers, a Non-Executive Directors community, recruitment and marketing agencies have come together to launch Tech Link Ukraine, an online resource to connect displaced Ukrainian technologists with organisations in Europe, particularly Ireland and the UK, that need technologist team members.

Tech Link Ukraine was created as business technology leaders were appalled by the invasion of Ukraine by Russia on 22 February 2022, and the suffering inflicted on Ukrainian society: "Our mission is to support technologists displaced by the war in Ukraine by providing the opportunity to work and support their families and loved ones."

The founding organisations behind Tech Link Ukraine aim to provide employment to displaced Ukrainian technologists, connecting their networks and opportunities to ensure Ukrainian technologists are able to work and support one another.

Organisations involved include CCO and talent acquisition leader Neil Dunwoody in Ireland, the Horizon CIO Network, UK IT Leaders, Virtualnonexecs.com, workforce software provider ProFinda, Penningtons Manches Cooper LLP immigration lawyer Pat Saini, and agile business-to-business marketing agency Bright.

Chief Information Officer (CIO) members represent organisations such as medical research funding body Wellcome, Times Higher Education, agricultural genomics research firm Synomics, and leading interim CIOs and change management experts Dave Jones, Shaun Taylor and Adrian Wakefield.

Neil Dunwoody says: "We are able to promote and drive practical support. The recruitment piece is the easy piece as the jobs are there." He added that a number of Irish, UK and international organisations have pledged their support.

The invasion of Ukraine and displacement of its citizens has been especially moving for the technology community. There has been a close and growing relationship between Ukraine and the technology industry. Ukraine's technology sector revenue has been growing over 25% year-on-year. Prior to the invasion, Ukraine was home to 200,000 developers, with 20,000 technology graduates leaving Ukrainian universities a year. Technology has become one of Ukraine's top three exports in a very short time, and had contributed 8% of the nation's gross domestic product (GDP).

"The next wave of innovation will come from Eastern Europe, from Ukraine in particular," wrote Dominique Piotet, CEO at UNIT.City, an innovation park in Kyiv, in 2021.

How to help

Tech Link Ukraine has three channels of help. The first is the ability for Ukrainian technologists looking for work to register themselves. The recruitment network supporting Tech Link Ukraine will contact them and begin the process of finding work. For business and technology leaders looking for technology talent, the second channel is an opportunity to register that you are able to support and recruit Ukrainian technologists.

A third channel enables organisations to donate technology or resources to support refugees with the ability to remain connected.

A number of charities have been contacted, and discussions on how to get connectivity to the refugees they are supporting are beginning to take place.

To help your peers in Ukraine, contact info@techlinkukraine.org or visit Tech Link Ukraine (https://techlinkukraine.org/).

Mark Chillingworth
European business writer specialising in technology leadership and chair of the Horizon CIO Network

Avril - Innovation and inventions come in all shapes and sizes. With an identified need and purpose what you need next is tenacity and hard work to find a way through.

Eileen - At Wellcome Trust in London there is a museum called Wellcome Collection that is open to members of the public. It hosts inspiring exhibitions, global events, and has plentiful curious, historical, and important artefacts on display to enjoy and interact with.

Covid-19 drove a change to how museums across the UK worked, and Wellcome Collection was no exception to that.

Driven by the need to make the museum space safe from Covid so that it could re-open its doors, the end-to-end visitor experience of the museum was reviewed including any displays and exhibits that members of the public had to touch for interaction.

Museums may traditionally have a bit of a reputation as 'please do not touch' environments and the following may be familiar to you:

Want to watch a video or listen to some audio? Wear these headphones.

Want to choose which track to play? Press one of these buttons.
Want to look through a slideshow of images? Swipe away on this iPad.

Want to play this game? Here are your joystick and buttons.
And the list goes on.

How to tackle this problem? Well, through technology of course.

With their endless enthusiasm and can-do attitude, the in-house audio-visual production team were keen to use technology in creative ways to solve this problem and enable the museum to open its doors to the public again.

It was not until the team started to tackle this, that they realised the true scale of the undertaking and just how reliant the Wellcome Collection was on touch for any kind of interaction. This project was going to require an entirely new way of thinking about the experience and back-to-the-drawing-board rethinking in how people interacted with the museum's exhibitions.
They met several obstacles along this road. For example, the specific requirements of Wellcome's Gallery spaces meant there was little in the way of 'off the shelf' solutions available. All this did, however, was spur the team on to create solutions and invent new uses for technology.

Having the space to design and test the solutions was also an obstacle during lockdown due to limited building access, and the team could often be found prototyping and testing new systems at home. They have some delightful stories of kitchen tables being awash with a sea of cables and components for weeks on end as they developed robust solutions to complex problems.

After weeks of long days designing and testing and inventing, the audio-visual production team successfully re-engineered how the public interacted with the museum exhibitions and artefacts through technology, and they designed equipment and technology to be used in ways it had never been used before.

For example, they installed headphone sockets for a bring-your-own headphones approach that detected when the cable was inserted and would start to playback.

They also used an infra-red trigger (just like automatic taps) to control the lighting in a display case and start video playback, instead of people using buttons to activate it.

They replaced standard buttons with footswitches that allowed people with limited hand dexterity the opportunity to use their feet.

They implemented the use of wireless real-time 3D modelling of people's hands for more sophisticated controls.

They even created a touch-free gesture control interaction from invisible sensors that allows a member of the public to scroll through a gallery of images simply by waving their hands.

As the team fondly describe it, "a little bit of audio-visual magic."

Whilst the driver for this was to be Covid-safe by removing touch from the exhibits, this fantastic use of technology and being creative in problem solving results in a fully inclusive experience of Wellcome Collection, and is a fitting example of how technology has been used to make things better for us all.

This story is accredited to Jeremy Bryans, Audio-visual and Multimedia Producer at Wellcome Trust, who worked (ridiculously hard) with his colleagues across Wellcome developing and installing these solutions.

Eileen Jennings-Brown
Top 50 Most Influential Women in the UK Tech.
Head of Technology for the Wellcome Trust

Avril - Feeling inspired by Wellcome's story and fancy inventing? Here are some great golden nuggets to start your thinking.

Let's share
wisdom!

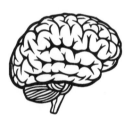

*"Design for how others want to use it
not how you think it should work."*

Stuart Duthie
CIO / CTO - Delivering Qualocity
(Pace, Direction and Quality) in Technology

*"If you're not failing,
you're not innovating."*

Danny Attias
Chief Digital and Information Officer

*"The answer isn't with me.
The answer isn't with you.
The answer is between us."*

Adrian Wakefield
CEO Transforming IT

*"To Quote Kobe B:
'Hard work beats talent when
talent fails to work hard.'"*

Dominic Hilleard
NED and Director of Executive Search

"Startup is hard! Ditch the mask, seek trusted advice and make time for those who are in similar positions. Being honest about the challenge is crucial."

Jonathan Wood
CEO and Founder at C2 Cyber Ltd

"Dream. Aim. Design. Deliver - always ambitious, assertive, agile, adaptable and an ambassador."

Chris Dadd
CEO DADD.TV, Innovating for good

"If I've asked for a cupcake don't bring me a Black Forest gateau."

Dave Jones
Fractional CIO and Chair of UK IT Leaders

"Aim high and dream big. Don't let yourself or anyone hold you back."

Tania Ferreira
Head of Event Content Production for the global DiversityQ
'Women In' Summit and Awards Series at Bonhill Media UK Ltd

Avril - Here we are dreaming big, thanks Tania. I am extremely good at going wild with my dreams, in fact maybe a bit too good. It tends to be my form of escapism. What happens if…? However, in reality, after the glamourous lights, the excitement and energy comes a long, long lull - the hurdles, the tears, the doubts, and repeat. So, how do we keep going? What fuel do we use? Thank goodness for friends and family, but don't forget to eat.

Chapter 3
Eat

To stop is relief
And a little bit fun,
But after a while
Wish to see someone.

Avril Chester

Avril - Are we nearly there yet? Am I doing the right thing? What have I taken on? Does the merry-go-round stop? This is the time to dig deep. This is the time to find your own fuel. It is very easy to wish to ignore the last few years, but through the pandemic there are incredible stories of resilience, so how can we not share these? We all had the same yet such different experiences. Caroline and Mignon reflect and share their stories.

Caroline - There is so much potential to talk about when we consider the positive impact that technology has on our lives. Being a total geek since I can remember (I taught myself to code on my Commodore 64 waaaaay back) I get really excited about technology full stop and always jump ahead to a wonderful Utopian world where we balance human and machine to improve everyone's way of life. That said, I think it's the impact on the individual that can demonstrate the starkest potential of what technology can really do.

Being the extrovert that I am, the original lockdown hit me hard. My family are a massive source of support for me and despite the fact I live over 240 miles away from them we had always seen each other in person at least once a month. Like so many other people I felt like that was totally ripped from me overnight and I struggled. I was in an incredibly lucky position and had to recognise that my immediate family were with me and safe, we lived in the country and had access to a big garden and my dog demanding walking kept me active. But still I struggled.

What made the biggest difference to me was the ability not just to speak to them, but to see them, to share those calls across my sisters so we could talk as a group and not as individuals. To physically see Dad and check on how he looked and not have to rely on the stoic 'I'm fine' message that I could guarantee I would get to the question 'how are you?'. This wasn't earth shattering tech that we used, it was pretty much things that we took for granted before I needed it so much.

That's why I wanted to focus on that as the technology that has made a positive impact. We can spend so much time thinking about massive changes and the far-reaching impact of technology that we miss the little things, the personally important things that get someone through a hard time that we shouldn't forget. There is such a massive range in the scale of the positive impact of technology and that's what I find really exciting.

Caroline Carruthers
Author, Chief Executive, Data Cheerleader

Mignon - I was working for a healthcare company during the pandemic, teams were feeling a little disconnected from each other and I was asked to set up a virtual technology women's network to help support morale and keep the ladies connected. We looked at technology options available and MS Teams was widely used at the organisation. As a starter I pulled a presentation together and highlighted all the successes of each of the ladies for that year and what absolute stars they were. After the presentation, the team reflected on how it cheered up their week and made them feel a little more connected.

Also, we set up a MS Teams group with shared interests on books, recipes, music, ideas, and also made use of quizzes to keep us connected and engaged during lockdown. Having a virtual collaboration/chat platform allowed us all to be in touch with each other and combat some of the loneliness and isolation during lockdown.

Mignon Mapplebeck
UK CIO who loves to inspire and motivate others

Avril - All organisations adjusted and we know technology doesn't need to cost the earth to bring a big impact to people's lives as demonstrated by Mignon and also by Christelle at Arsenal FC.

Christelle - Much has been written about the negative aspects of technology, such as distorted imagery impacting the self-esteem of our teenagers and bias creeping into artificial intelligence. However, few people would dispute that technology can also be a huge source of good in society.

It is always the human stories of how technology can have a positive impact on people's lives that resonate with me the most. Only when I started working for a Premier League football club could I say that I truly understood how central football can be to people's lives. For some, supporting a team can be like belonging to a tribe. For them, nothing is more thrilling than being at a live match alongside thousands of other of their tribal members. But of course, in 2020, as the pandemic spiralled out of control, football matches were played in stadiums bereft of fans...

Whilst many people suffered with isolation during the lockdown, I could imagine that many disabled fans may have felt this more acutely without their regular trips to see their team play. Arsenal FC really cares for its disabled fans and goes out of its way to ensure they have an enjoyable experience at the Emirates Stadium in non-pandemic times.

I will always remember a few months into lockdown being approached by the gentleman with responsibility for disabled fans. He had this great idea to try and create the atmosphere of their supporters' lounge in the Emirates before a match, but virtually. Not knowing where to start, he asked if I could help. At that time, Microsoft Teams was in full use across the Club for meetings. It took little effort to create a group in Teams for his fans then ensure he was fully comfortable with all relevant functionality. After a brief test with a smaller group of fans, he was all set for the next match! He had created a virtual space for the fans to 'meet' before, during and after the match. Somewhere to watch the match together, chat together, and support their team.

So, this wasn't about leading edge technology, or a complex, large, time-consuming or expensive project (as IT projects often can be!). Neither was there a multi-million pound return on investment. But a small amount of effort yielded a large amount of satisfaction, not just for the fans, and they wouldn't have known it, but for me too. It always brings a smile to my face when I remember that I played a small part in helping recreate some of the camaraderie those fans were missing being unable to attend live matches. And at a time when it was surely more important than ever.

Christelle Heikkila
Technology Leader and Non-Executive Director

Avril - The one thing we all have in common is our health and I am so personally thankful to everyone involved in this space. The speed of technology delivery in healthcare over the last few years has been truly remarkable, just like Rachel and the Difrent team. You are all epic.

**How Difrent delivered the Covid testing programme
in just eight days.**

Rachel - Delivering the UK's biggest ever home testing programme was a huge ask, full stop. But delivering it in a week? Almost impossible. When NHSX approached Difrent and asked us to deliver a home test ordering service in seven days we were aware it was going to be a massive undertaking. But the NHS was buckling under Covid pressures and around 40% of staff were in isolation due to unconfirmed symptoms, so we got to work.

Fortunately, Difrent is used to working quickly. When I joined the company it focused solely on recruitment, with just two permanent staff. But as my experience is in service delivery, we quickly rebranded ourselves to provide public sector support services, and in just six months we had secured our first major contract with the NHS.

When Covid took hold, it made sense that we would turn our expertise to the delivery of the testing programme and play our role in supporting the NHS. In total, it took us eight days to design the testing service from scratch and deliver it to the first group of NHS staff.

Over the course of three months, one million home test kits were delivered in the UK. Here's how we did it.

On the first day we interviewed more than 50 service stakeholders remotely, mapped the service blueprint and set the project goals. Over the next four days we focused on developing the service architecture, creating the contact centre guides and set up the website. By day eight the first staff at London Ambulance Service were able to order test kits online, which has to be our proudest achievement to date.

Of course, the work didn't stop once the programme went live. We documented the experiences of LAS staff using the tests, set up an assisted digital contact centre to support people who had accessibility needs, and analysed user performance data. This allowed us to adapt the testing programme for everyone in the UK, rather than just key workers, and have it ready for the entire population in the space of six weeks.

Those were an incredibly gruelling six weeks, and we are hugely proud of the achievement, not just within the coronavirus programme but also highlighting how tech can be used to solve large scale problems in healthcare. The role digital has to play in healthcare can sometimes be unclear with negative connotations – as clinicians are often plagued by clunky and out of date IT systems.

On the flip side the idea of health tech can be over-complicated and only associated with things like fancy AI work and 3D printing.

However, our rapid launch of the Covid testing programme shows the major practical benefits tech can have in healthcare, especially if the NHS is supported in the right way.

Rachel Murphy
CEO of Difrent. Advisor and Investor in Healthtech companies. On a
personal mission to contribute towards global health equity for all.

Avril - Absolutely brilliant! Wasn't the vaccine programme amazing? The sheer speed and scale begin to prove anything is possible. To put an ask out there, could we coordinate something like this, the huge, targeted energy at scale for cancer please? Thank you, Chris Lewis, (diagnosed with Stage 4 Mantle Cell Lymphoma, a rare blood cancer) for all the campaigning you do. You are fabulous, formidable and I feel blessed to be able to call you my friend.

*"You can no longer afford
to be a passive patient."*

Chris Lewis @christheeagle1
Chris Cancer Community and COO of SimPal

Avril - Like many, I am on repeat prescriptions and with osteoporosis accelerated because of cancer treatment, I leave the pharmacy with a big bag full of goodies. It's not quite the same as an exciting pic 'n' mix, but I like to pretend it is. The pandemic interrupted supply chains, this included ingredients for medicines. My Tamoxifen supplier (hormone therapy for breast cancer) fast ran out of stock. Just use another supplier of Tamoxifen, I hear you say. Well, it's not that easy. Each supplier uses different ingredients, these have different side effects. After creating a table of well-known brands, I could see the same two or three ingredients with even more, at least six or seven, different to the one I currently use. This is hormone treatment. Being five years in to my 10-year intake, I have learned how to handle the side effects.

I was scared. I feared catching Covid. Cancer already took a year of my life and I'm in no mood to be seriously ill again, thank you very much. But I was also scared of handling drug-induced hormone changes while living alone, being locked inside the house with work going bonkers and emotions running high.

Step forward my incredible pharmacy. They were and are an absolute lifeline. They found 10mg instead of 20mg boxes. At every opportunity, whenever a small amount became available from the supplier, they'd pre-order and store out back for when my prescription arrived. They found every way possible to keep me going. From the bottom of my heart, thank you.

We can only make decisions based on the information we have available at that given time. What was challenging was finding advice on how the vaccine behaved with repeat prescriptions. With the news packed full of horror stories about blood clots, I emailed my surgeon, who in turn spoke to the oncologist, who in turn advised that Macmillan had just updated their website with advice on the vaccine with medication. I asked Declan what it was like from his side.

Macmillan's Covid Hub.

Declan - During Covid we realised we needed to create a reliable source of information for patients with cancer. With so little information, it was important to quickly develop reliable clinical information to support the hundreds of thousands of people with cancer in the UK who had questions. The internet is full of information with not all of it good and it was imperative we created the trusted source of information we knew was essential.

Macmillan launched their first Corona Virus information on 11 March 2020, launched the Corona Virus hub on 25 March 2020 with the patient personalisation on 21 April 2020. Getting initial information and the hub up in a matter of days, and personalisation within weeks, was an amazing achievement and included a number of offerings:

- Specific clinical information for Corona Virus and cancer.
- By answering a few multiple-choice questions, creating a personalised guide on Corona Virus and cancer. https://www. macmillan.org.uk/coronavirus/cancer-and-coronavirus-guide
- Ability to register as a volunteer to befriend a cancer patient during the pandemic as we assessed the level of loneliness would be a challenge for those diagnosed. This was a really successful initiative.
- In a month we would see over 100,000 page views on our Corona Virus hub alone.
- The Macmillan Corona Virus hub was mentioned in Parliament as the reliable source of cancer information for patients during the pandemic.

The information was updated daily by using agile techniques developed as part of the digital transformation programme that I led.

Declan Hunt
Technology and Digital professional who specialises in supporting organisations through significant transformational change. Following a career as a successful CIO in organisations such as Macmillan Cancer Support and G4S, he is now a freelance consultant specialising in digital and technology transformation. Declan is also a Trustee of the London Irish Centre.

Avril - The power of technology and science in all its brilliant glory. Moving thoughts onto politics, how did the Houses of Commons and Lords continue? What impact did technology bring to the governing bodies of our country? Thank you, Tracey, to you and your teams for providing an essential service and congratulations on winning the 2021 Women in IT, Outstanding Contribution of the Year award.

Tracey - In response to the Covid-19 pandemic, the Houses of Commons and Lords agreed to introduce virtual participation in debates to allow for social distancing and help prevent the spread of the virus. They also introduced remote voting in divisions. As at January 2022 the House of Commons has removed virtual participation, and evolved remote voting into a permanent system of electronic pass reader voting in its division lobbies. In the House of Lords, arrangements have been made to continue virtual participation for eligible Members with long-term disabilities, enabling them to participate in Chamber or Grand Committee remotely and to vote electronically or by telephone whether on or off the Parliamentary Estate. Proposals for a permanent system of electronic pass reader voting, again located in division lobbies, have been published and will be debated in the House of Lords, and its committees are able to choose whether to meet in person, hybrid or virtually.

Research undertaken by the House of Lords Library[1] showed some interesting differences between wholly physical, virtual and hybrid

---

[1] https://lordslibrary.parliament.uk/house-of-lords-impact-of-virtual-and-hybrid-sittings-in-2020/

participation in the House of Lords in 2020 and pointed to the fact that before the introduction of virtual proceedings, member participation in the Chamber and in Grand Committee had been falling since the beginning of the pandemic. For example:

• In the last five sitting days before the introduction of virtual proceedings (13–19 March 2020), the average number of members speaking each day was 23 fewer than for the average of the same period in the previous three years.
• The average number of spoken contributions each day was 51 fewer than for the same time in the previous three years.

The introduction of virtual proceedings led to changes in member participation:

• There was an increase in the number of members speaking each day. Between 21 April 2020 and 4 June 2020, the average number speaking each day was 29 more than for the same time in the previous three years.

• The average number of spoken contributions each day was 35 fewer than for the same time in the previous three years. This meant that, while more members were speaking, they made fewer contributions on each day on average. This may have been the result of members speaking virtually not being able to make interventions.

Hybrid proceedings, where some Members were able to participate in the Chamber while observing social distancing and others contributed remotely, saw an increase in member participation compared to previous years, both in terms of the number of members speaking and the number of spoken contributions:

• From 8 June 2020 to the end of the year, the average number of members speaking each day was 32 more than for the same time over the previous three years.

• The average number of spoken contributions each day was 84 more than for the same time over the previous three years.

Any comparison between two periods of House of Lords activity is difficult because of the many variables involved. For example, there are potentially large differences in the types of business taking place and the length of any sittings involved.

What had become clear though was that Lords Members who might be physically unable to attend the House on grounds of long-term disability had been able to use virtual proceedings to participate virtually in the work of the House of Lords. The House of Lords Procedure and Privileges Committee suggested: "It is vital that the House should continue to benefit from the perspectives of disabled Members"[2] and following discussion on the floor of the House of Lords it was agreed to introduce Standing Order No 24a meaning disabled Peers can apply for eligible member status and if granted they may choose to participate virtually in proceedings in the Chamber or in Grand Committee, and to vote remotely.

At Parliament, and probably all big organisations, progress is not always linear, and the most elegant of digital solutions don't always suit the business in the long-term. Some of the things which had to be introduced during a pandemic context changed the character of the Chambers, removing spontaneous interventions on speeches, something which has been a famous feature of the UK Parliament. This doesn't take away from the achievements of the digital teams at Parliament in the pandemic, and the

---

[2] Procedure and Privileges Committee, 4th Report of Session 2021-22, Speakers' lists for oral questions and
'Secretary of State' questions Divisions: passreader

recognition of the inclusion benefits for disabled Peers from the House of Lords is a welcome outcome.

Tracey Jessup
Chief Digital & Information Officer at the UK Parliament

Avril - Life also presented the opportunity for a burst of new initiatives, ideas, and startups. Let's invent! Could I be bold and call it a renaissance of creativity? There were amazing personal projects of discovery and the introduction of a new word in my vocabulary; 'sondership'.

Danny - In the summer of 2021, I launched a podcast called Sondership with the tagline, Inspiring Stories from People with Purpose. Each week I would interview guests who were driven to have a positive impact on society. Season One ran for 22 episodes and covered a diverse spectrum of guests from the UK, the US, Africa and Asia, each with their own story, their own purpose and their own motivations.

As a Chief Digital and Information Officer, previously with the stem cell register Anthony Nolan, saving the lives of people with blood cancer, and more recently with London Business School, which seeks to have a profound impact on the way the world does business and the way business impacts the world, it was inevitable that many of my guests were from the field of technology and were using technology to create good. I wanted to inspire others by sharing their real, raw and honest stories to show how achievable their accomplishments could be to you or me. They had simply blended their inspiration, confronted their imposter moments and harnessed whatever privilege they had to influence positive change.

This project came about through a combination of inspiration and a trigger. The trigger was the discovery of a new word 'sonder', coined by John Koenig in his Dictionary of Obscure Sorrows and defined as "the realisation that each random passer by is living a life as vivid and complex as your own." How often do we stop, step out of our own heads and our own stories and look out onto all of the other stories playing out around us? And not just look, but really see other people as a whole, not just for the glancing overlap with your story but for all the things that make them whole.

My inspiration came from a handful of incredible people, many of whom I have been lucky enough to have as guests on Sondership with the hope that their stories will inspire others as they did for me. Most notable is Avril Chester, an impressive technology leader in her own right, but also the founder of Cancer Central, the charity to which this book is donating its proceeds. She's a cancer thriver who combined her first hand experience of an awful disease and her sharp technology skills to create an information service that she felt was missing when she needed it most.

I would encourage everyone to pause every now and then, reflect on what social injustice really resonates for them, consider their privileges, and not just affluence, it may be their unique perspective, their social network, their special skills or talents and then overcome those imposter moments that plague all of us, in order to have a positive impact in the world.

Danny Attias
Chief Digital and Information Officer

Avril - Too kind Danny, honestly it's just me. I can't cook for toffee, or garden for that matter. I accidentally killed a cactus just before Christmas.

It was a Father Christmas cactus so you can imagine how long I'd had it for and it died before Christmas Day. How can you kill a cactus? Raw, green-fingered talent, that's me, and as for cooking, please don't ever ask me to be sous-chef, just ask my friends if you don't believe me. I thoroughly enjoy the talents of anyone who wishes to cook for me. Talking of which I went to my first in-person event the other week. Leaving the nervousness aside, the food, oh the food! How I have missed you! A plate presented as art with melt in the mouth experiences. Funnily enough, my microwave extravaganzas don't quite look or taste the same. I wonder why. ;-)

What to eat? A common question for me, but in all seriousness, here are some fabulous golden nuggets to help re-fuel.

Let's share
wisdom!

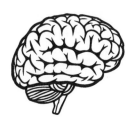

"Embrace the experiment!"

Chris B Lord
Group CTO at Babcock International,
driving information exploitation and innovation

"Stand up for yourself and others."

Tania Ferreira
Head of Event Content Production for the global
DiversityQ 'Women In' Summit and Awards
Series at Bonhill Media UK Ltd

"It is better to do something and regret it than not do it and regret it."

Stephen Johnson
CEO ROQ

"Know yourself well... your values, principles and what keeps you contented and centred. Once you know that, challenges in your personal and work life are so much easier to deal with."

Sandhya Sharma
HR and Lecturer, a keen observer of life

"Carpe Diem - seize the day. There are no outer limits."

Mathew Mallett
Chief Digital and Information Officer, UK Space
Agency and Chief Operating Officer Cancer Central

"Forget trying to feel confident. It's a temporary state at best and it's entirely contextual. If something makes you nervous it's almost certainly a sign that you'll grow from the experience. Seek discomfort some of the time. Change the narrative from 'I feel nervous' to 'I'm excited to....' and feel the smile break through as you say that word."

Claire Priestley
CDIO, Founder CIO+1, Co-Founder The Secret
Boxing Gym, believer in the awesomeness of people

Avril - For those who listen to our podcast the 3 Digital Amigos, you know that Craig, Chris and I always try to wrangle something about food into every episode for a bit of fun. Surely then I couldn't leave food out of this book? This one is for you podcast listeners. Craig, Chris, hope my food reference here has made you proud.

Anyone else struggling with half their wardrobe post lockdown? Here's an extra poem for us all.

Eat

I shouldn't
But I must,
Bread or olives
Leave the crust.

The juices
What to drink,
Water or wine
Just one clink.

It's no fun
Leaving the rum,
Soup or prawns
Hand the pecans.

Think diet
Triple cooked chips,
Meat or vegetarian
All on the hips.

It's not fair
Why do cakes stare,
Biscuit or mint
What if I squint?

-

Avril Chester

Chapter 4
Boost

*I'm in a tizzle
What a tuzzle,
All is a fizzle
What a fuzzle.*

Avril Chester

Avril - Out of sorts, flat as a pancake? Doesn't have to be triggered by something big, could be your programme funding has been pulled, your product launch didn't quite hit the mark, you sent an email you didn't mean to, or the weather is a continual cloud of dark grey drizzle. We all need a little pick-me-up at times, a smile, a motivational moment. I hope this chapter does just that and there is no better way to start than to read how people are making a difference, like the amazing and inspirational Ezechi.

Ezechi - I've always loved technology, it was the power to create whole worlds that attracted me to it originally, playing arcade video games as a child at my local swimming club I was inescapably drawn to the colours, the action the pure creativity and imagination on show.

So it's no surprise that when I could I learnt how to programme and I've never looked back since. Learning to code took me from a failed A-level student, to a coder in an investment bank, to a fintech founder, to an investor in startups, to an MBE. It's safe to say that technology levelled me up dramatically. These tech skills are what have enabled me to succeed in the way that I have. But I love how it's opened up doors for others also.

At Code Untapped we run hackathons where the aim is to showcase the skills of diverse and under-represented technologists by partnering with companies and giving the companies the chance to see these diverse techies in action. Over the years we have run many of these events but one always sticks out in my mind.

One of the hackathons that we ran was for the Department for Education (DfE). The focus of it was to provide a more suitable portal for teachers who are searching for jobs. The event we ran was a one-day hack and we had over 30 people from all sorts of backgrounds turn up.

Each team had to identify the core ask of the day, think of a solution, put together a prototype, and pitch it to a judging panel with the prize being that the winning team would have the opportunity to take their idea and pitch it to a panel of senior managers from the DfE at its head office near Westminster Abbey.

The winning team did an excellent job pitching their idea, but the surprise came when we started speaking to the team about their backgrounds. Incredibly, one of our finalists was a Korean nurse who had never spent a day coding before!

He had found out about our event the day before the hackathon, decided to join at the last minute and couldn't believe that he had now had the opportunity to pitch a tech idea in Westminster! I like to think that he is now busy working on his next idea and getting ready to pitch for investment funding with a view to going global!

This is the true power of technology, the ability for normal people to take ideas and turn them into an actual product with the potential to reach a worldwide audience.

Technologists are modern-day alchemists, instead of lead we take ideas and turn them into gold. Sometimes those ideas fail but that's the great thing about tech, there are always more ideas, always more code that can be written, more technologies to create.

I hope these stories inspire more people like our Korean nurse to learn to code and to become technologists. I can't wait to see the future that they will create.

Ezechi Britton MBE
From Developer to Co-Founder and CTO, to Serial Entrepreneur and
VC. It's been quite a journey!

Avril - I love that, 'sometimes those ideas fail but that's the great thing'. Let's keep giving ourselves a boost and read how Dr Jacqui came to focus on a world in which we leave no one behind.

Welcome to the Empathy Economy.

Dr Jacqui - I'm sharing part of my technology career journey, and what led me to create the technology for the Empathy Economy I founded: to enable a world founded on inclusion, a world where we leave no one behind.

I'm Dr Jacqui Taylor, CEO and co-founder of FlyingBinary. We are a company founded by two engineers who have pioneered the web science and engineering needed to build the deep technology for the Empathy Economy.

In 2009, with 249 other London entrepreneurs, we created Tech City, the first virtual city on Earth. I am also the co-founder of the data journalism industry, where an ecosystem of over seven million journalists use data to tell evidence-based stories to the world. You will have heard of Panama, Paradise, and Pandora Papers, I'm sure. If you are one of the 34 million citizens who consume the data stories FlyingBinary creates, stay tuned. We will be launching the Empathy Economy's next steps very soon.

I didn't start my technology journey as a career choice. I failed my exams because I was caring for my mum in the final stages of an aggressive cancer. I left school at 16 to keep my family together and my summer internship at a local aerospace company became the first step in my career path.

Aged 17, I was offered a full time apprenticeship, which involved study two nights a week and all day Saturday, alongside attempting the impossible, to step into Mum's shoes. A strong work ethic runs through my Irish heritage so that is what I did, aerospace engineering was going to be my future. It worked, I got my degree, won the college prize, the rest of my family was intact, and the prospect of a bright engineering future beckoned.

For the second time in my career, life intervened. The idea of a woman being part of an engineering team to build the aircraft to solve noise pollution for cities across the world was a step too far. Instead, I was offered a job in the computing department. That Irish work ethic kicked in again, but with an added mission: I wanted to use technology to solve the big problems for society. Could it do that? I was planning to find out.

After successful technology transitions for the UK clearing system after repeated unsuccessful attempts, I was the first ever technologist to deploy across the whole of the UK's National Health Service. I was part of the team to deregulate the UK's energy supply industry by which time I knew enough to successfully deploy technology in any sector, at scale. However, these projects didn't deliver tangible benefits to society. So where next?

When our son was eight, he was given a standard assessment by his school, which evidenced visual dyspraxia, a learning difference that wasn't understood and didn't have a good prognosis for his future at school, or in life. As a family, we resolved to work with the professionals we met, to contribute our technology skills to support this new cohort of young people who learned differently. Starting with just six pupils, through to a cohort of 1,000, we created the technology to support this and many other learning differences.

In 2009, I contributed my knowledge at a gathering of research specialists at the Royal Society, convened by Sir Tim Berners-Lee. FlyingBinary was formed that day.

Eight years later, our pioneering web science work had identified how our technology could be used to unlock the talents of the cohort we had supported from the beginning: Gen Z. Gen Z are our web entrepreneurs, and they influenced over 40% of economic spend in 2020. FlyingBinary has now positively impacted over half the world's population with our work.

At Davos 2019, I announced that we were pivoting our deep technology to support the new generation of entrepreneurs, GenAlpha. This cohort also includes some GenBeta entrepreneurs, the youngest of which is just five years old! If you are raising one of these young people, technology is a tool that will bring their talents to the world.

I founded the Empathy Economy in Tech City in London in 2016 to prepare our company for Brexit. I was in conversation with some of the

Tech City entrepreneurs who were with us when we started the FlyingBinary inclusion journey in 2009 and realised it was time to share the technology we had built as an enabler to an inclusive society.

So far, we have welcomed over 100 million entrepreneurs to the Empathy Economy, from every country in the world. We are working to deliver a Net Zero agenda, and we would love you to join us. The waitlist for the next cohort of Empathy Economy businesses is open, and you can join us at https://jacqui.online/waitlist.

A final word about my mum, who had a positive impact on our own community in the days before the web was created. Crowds lined the funeral route to say goodbye, and there were too many people to fit into the crematorium building.

I've dedicated my contribution to this book to my amazing mum, Joan Hardman. In 16 short years, she gave me a foundation that many of our young people today aren't given. The Empathy Economy, and the enabling Deep Technology we build, delivers inclusion and is bringing the talents of all young people to the world, leaving no one behind.

Dr Jacqui Taylor
CEO, co-Founder FlyingBinary

Avril - Sadly lost someone special? For Joan and those we have lost in our lives. Thank you, Dr Jacqui. Two very inspirational people. Remember we each have our strengths. Write yours down now. Yes, write on this page, remember you are incredible because you are unique. I bet there are many people who find you inspirational, yes, they do. To help, start by writing down your achievements from the last year, however small or large. We easily forget our achievements because we constantly assess what we are yet to do (guilty as charged) so this story about perceptions from Trevor made me smile so much.

Trevor - Thirty years ago, in the 1990s, I was working for one of the largest and most well-known Japanese security firms in the world. I was based in London and responsible for all aspects of technology - although in those days the job title was Head of Data Processing. That was because we had a hodgepodge of different and disparate systems that required lots of manual input and reinput. We had Wang VS word processors for the secretaries, Unix based trading support systems, PCs running Windows 3.1 for the quants, and mainframes to send the data back to Tokyo.

After working there for a few years, out of the blue I received a fax from Tokyo head office sent from the Head of the Systems Planning department: "Dear Trevor san, we are carrying out a review of all our global offices systems as part of strategic planning for the future. Please could you send us information about the systems in London?" Great, I thought, finally we can get some significant investment in our systems, and we can leverage the far superior capabilities that exist in the firm globally rather than what I am trying to do here in London. So, in response, I prepared a detailed memo (remember those?) and faxed back to Tokyo for input into their planning. I waited patiently, but silence. Eventually, I forgot about it and was back into the groove of day-to-day support.

The following year, the fax reappeared: "Dear Trevor san, we are carrying out a review of all our global offices systems as part of strategic planning for the future. Please could you send us information about the systems in London?" Wait, did they receive my message last year? I used some of my Japanese colleagues in London to verify that was the case and so thought maybe this planning is taking so long they want to be sure they know very latest status of where their plans will be implemented - great foresight Tokyo Systems Planning department, you clearly know what you are doing, I thought. I duly got the previous year's memo out and updated it with the latest things we had implemented - a Novel Netware network and structured cabling - but these would be insignificant I thought compared to the grand plans of Tokyo. Having sent the updated memo by fax, I waited patiently but again silence.

Year 3, the fax reappeared again: "Dear Trevor san, we are carrying out a review of all our global offices systems as part of strategic planning for the future. Please could you send us information about the systems in London?" We had rolled out MS Office in London since the previous year, together with Lotus cc:Mail. Great, I thought, let's update the memo into a PowerPoint presentation with diagrams and email it to Tokyo. Wait, there's no email address in Tokyo, so I had to fax it instead. But once again, silence. This process repeated for the next three years. Same outcome each year, silence.

But then, finally, as part of an international corporate cultural awareness programme I was invited to Tokyo to meet my counterparts. At last, I thought, I can meet the leaders of the Systems Planning department and discuss their plans, and understand when they will impact London. I was very enthusiastic. So, after the longest flight I'd ever had and a week in an offsite training facility where I learnt about Japanese culture, I was then in the head office of my company.

Japan has always portrayed the image of being very hi-tech / futuristic and I thought to myself how fortunate I was to glimpse how the future strategy of the company would play out in London. I talked to some of the management and asked them where I would find the Systems Planning department. "It's not here in the HQ, it's above a 7-11 convenience store two blocks away," they said.

Slightly odd, I thought, but I left the head office to find them. True enough, after walking two blocks, I found the 7-11 store and true enough at the back of the store was an elevator, labelled 'Systems Planning Department'. Here it is, I thought, at last, a chance to see future plans and be amazed. After a short ride to the top of the building, the doors opened to a large open plan office. Desks were orderly laid out in rows and shelves bordered the room. There was a single mainframe terminal screen in the middle of the room, all the desks appeared to just have paper files on them and no technology devices.

My illusions of hi-tech Japan were suddenly smashed when I realised the single screen was for the whole team and usage had to be booked. And then, looking at the shelves around the room I saw the 'London' shelf and on it a lever arch file with my memos and PowerPoints printed and translated. From what I could see and what I discussed there was no grand plan for a global systems strategy, and the Systems Planning department was nothing more than an information gatherer. I returned to London disappointed, but in some ways enthused about the level of systems I had delivered to the firm with very limited budget. So my advice is, don't wait for grand plans, do the best you can with what you have.

Trevor Hunt
CTO Advisory Behind Every Cloud, connecting your business to the
best technology providers

Avril - So, so true. Are you thinking about a career in tech? Perhaps a move into the industry or desire to learn more? In need of a little insight on what it is like? This one is for Kelly, take it away Kelly.

Kelly - You may call us the IT department, Digital, Tech, Data, Engineering, Infrastructure, Software or DevSecOps, I call us "My fellowship, my guild!"

My first introduction to the world of technology was through a wonderful data scientist, my mum! She, and my dad, bought me my first computer; a ZX Spectrum, in 1982. The iPhone 13 has over 100,000 more RAM than that early 'affordable' home computer. I spent hours playing computer games and wrote my first software on it. At school my interest was always piqued by STEM subjects, I love understanding how the world works. My school years were the early days of computing, education was light and considered the realm of the true geek. In my computer studies class, I was the only girl, which was never an issue for me, or my fellow students, but me being female seemed overly strange to our teacher.

At university I chose environmental sciences. Like many others, I loved my studies, but I hadn't joined them up to how my degree linked to a career.

After university, I got a temporary role in a software house and it was there I fell back in love with digital technology. Fresh faced and new to the world of working in an office, my role was to do anything to make office life better and more efficient for my colleagues (experience I still draw on as a leader). I tended reception, typed letters, covered the customer technology helpdesk, and booked flights for executives.

Of all the people I met, I was drawn to the software engineers. They were smart, interesting, interested and happy to teach me about their vocation. The development team were revered, and I liked them. I felt at home!

I sought out self-study. I learned about databases and programming, the logical structure really suited my brain and more and more I found that my fellow engineers were my type of people. This revered community opened its arms to me and welcomed me in. I joined an internal training programme and rotated through all of the disciplines of the technology department and my thirst to learn was greeted with generosity of colleagues who answered my questions, pointed me to resources, and I learned my craft.

I have never looked back. I am surrounded by polymaths, people with a talent for combining business knowledge with abstract logic. People who are able to hold multiple ideas in their head at the same time, a function where teamwork is essential. These people have been wonderful to me, generous, open, collaborative and fun. More than 20 years later and I am still passionate about being part of this community.

I found my fellowship!

*For anyone feeling they or a young adult needs to join the education and career dots, I urge you not to ponder on this for too long. Follow your heart, and study what makes you happy, you have your entire life to be a grown up and get serious. Learn the art of learning and you will go far!

Kelly Francis
I have an IT department in my head, and it's noisy in here

Avril - Mega, 'follow your heart'. My heart is there but I'm a little stuck, what's next and how do I unlock?

Zoe - Most people at some point in their career or life reach a point when they ask themselves, 'what next?'. For a lucky few, the answer to that question is easy, but for many of us it can remain unanswered, leading to inertia, frustration or discontent.

I am President of a company [Frank Recruitment Group] that helps thousands of technology professionals to find a new job. This is perhaps the most obvious way to answer that 'what next?' question but we know it isn't the only solution if you're looking for career fulfilment. Many of our candidates have found that having a mentor or being a mentor can provide them with a renewed sense of passion and purpose.

In 2021 we launched an initiative called Mentor Me that matches women across the technology industry with a more experienced professional in their field for a six-month programme of mentoring. Our first cohort featured 20 matched pairs, all from very different backgrounds and with very different expectations about what they hoped the programme might bring them. For some, it was about making their next career move but for others it was about making more of the role they were in, finding ways to hone their expertise, build their interpersonal skills, or even bring elements of an outside passion or hobby into their working life. Since the programme began, several of our mentees have started new roles or taken on new responsibilities. Others have gained valuable technical certifications. A couple have found new audiences for their blogs and posts about their experiences as women in tech and been invited to take part in seminars and podcasts as a result.

For many of our mentors, the experience has been just as rewarding – a way to make a difference and a reminder of the skills and experiences they can share.

If you are asking yourself, 'what next?' then I would encourage you to first ask 'what do I currently have?'. Mentoring can be a powerful way of taking stock. As one of our mentees put it: 'It has made me think about the hard questions and the even harder answers. It's a great experience to connect with other people, hear about amazing experiences and go home with great advice.'

Whether you're a mentee or mentor, the experience can help you build on the skills you have so when that next opportunity presents itself, you're ready.

Zoe Morris

Zoe Morris is President of Frank Recruitment Group,

leading technology resourcing

Avril - Thank you so much Zoe. Let's take her advice, ask yourself and write down, 'what do I currently have'?

I know every day tends to end up in a juggling competition and this can have a massive impact on our energy levels. There's lots of books on this topic but are there any practical tips which can give us a boost? Thank you Ahsan for sharing how you juggle.

Ahsan - It is ever more important in the current age to ensure our mental wellbeing is given the thought it duly requires.

On a personal note, having three young children, a business and lots of voluntary charity work presented an enormous pressure on life in general. And if not for the positive impact of technology, it would have been much more challenging to manage.

There are many ways of enhancing your mental wellbeing. The following recommendations are focused solely on how technologies such as Microsoft supported me with the day-to-day activities.

Leveraging Microsoft Teams to work flexibly, allowed me to balance personal commitments with my work agenda. Of course, these tips can be used across other platforms as well.

For the purpose of this piece, I will focus on the following wellbeing aspects:
- Mindful of me
- Mindful of others
- Managing time
- In the zone
- Minimise distractions
- Switching off

Mindful of Me

Set your own boundaries – Set quiet hours/ days in the Teams mobile app

While our mobiles have untied us from our desks, it can be a challenge when trying to switch off. You can set your own boundaries by configuring quiet hours and days in the Teams mobile app.

Track your wellbeing – monitor quiet days / after-hours activity in My Analytics

Remember to keep yourself in check by taking note of the Wellbeing insights you get in Outlook, delivered as part of MyAnalytics and see how you're tracking with your quiet days.

Mindful of Others

Delay after-hours emails

Some of us spend most of our days in meetings and therefore, spend our evenings catching up on emails. Be mindful of how this impacts your team, particularly if you're a manager. While you may not set the expectation to reply to the email, the simple act of reading will have an impact.

• Keep your after-hours impact in check by monitoring My Analytics.
• Consider delaying the delivery of your email (using the 'Delay Delivery' option in Outlook), this way you can still work in the way you like, whilst minimising the impact on others.

Record your meetings, make them inclusive

Think about those that can't make your meeting time, or like to learn at their own pace, record your team meetings

Managing Time

Schedule time to review emails, to learn and just get things done with Focus time

Leverage the insights from MyAnalytics to understand your current ways of working and whether there are areas that can help you become more efficient and productive. MyAnalytics can provide insights around your out of hours working, your top collaborators, recommendation on focus time, to actually get work done etc.

In the Zone

Set 'Do Not Disturb' in Teams

Prevent interruptions while working on critical tasks or projects by setting Do Not Disturb in Teams and prevent distractions, whilst still being able to get notifications from your pre-assigned priority (see 'Manage priority access' privacy settings in Teams).

Improve focus

Improve focus and comprehension by using immersive reader in Teams, Office and Edge. Reading comprehension of long documents is made easier when words are highlighted while read out loud. This feature is a great inclusive design tool for reading long, complicated text, when multi-tasking, or when you get tired at the end of the day.

Minimise Distractions

Maintain Focus

- Maintain focus on what really matters during the meeting, the people and the content being shared by removing any background noise using Background Effects in Microsoft Teams Meetings (Blur background).
- Encourage no device policy in meetings to promote full engagement.
- Prevent unnecessary distractions by disabling all social media notifications on your phone.

Switching Off

Work life balance is important

When you're on holiday, set your Out of Office automatic replies and stop syncing Outlook. Additionally, leave your laptop at home and feel empowered to remove work apps off your phone to avoid sneak peeking into your emails.

MS Teams: Top Productivity Tips

• Arrange your Teams in an order that makes sense to you, putting the busiest Teams at the top of your list, do this by selecting and dragging them.
• Pin your favourite channels at the top of the list.
• Keep on top of things through your activity feed.
• Use filter or type /unread in the search bar to see your unread channel notifications.
• Use filter or type /mentions in the search bar to see all your @ mentions.
• Save messages and find them easily later.

Ataur-Rahim Ahsan
Co-Founder and Technical Director @ SloopTech Ltd

Avril - Just what I needed, thank you for sharing, Ahsan. Let's finish this boost chapter with va va voom.

"Yes, you can."

Tiffany Willcox
Chief Technology Officer, Marie Curie

"Sometimes things go wrong but never stop believing in yourself."

Christelle Heikkila
Technology Leader and Non-Executive Director

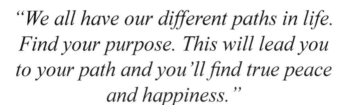

"We all have our different paths in life. Find your purpose. This will lead you to your path and you'll find true peace and happiness."

Sean Sadler
An IT Leader taking one day at a time

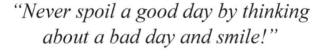

"Never spoil a good day by thinking about a bad day and smile!"

Niel Young
Seasoned Senior Test Analyst working for ROQ and
proud to be a part of the Cancer Central journey

"This too shall change so enjoy the successes and squeeze every last drop of value out of the failures."

Mark Harrison
Seasoned Change Agent and Technology Ambassador /
Leader / Advisor

"Let your life be like a beautiful night sky with an infinite amount of stars for opportunities, and the moon to help shine the light on your path."

Mignon Mapplebeck
UK CIO who loves to inspire and motivate others

"People often ask me about finding a mentor, or ask me to mentor them. Mentors are everywhere! Just observe people working around you, reflect on what you can learn from them and how you can apply it."

Melanie Rose
Senior Leader in IT Delivery and Service Management

Avril - Thanks Melanie for that top tip. We're four chapters in and let's shift gears. Grab those Post-its, this is advance notice. It's time to embrace change.

Chapter 5
Change

I'm out of range
Feels a bit strange,
Ready to exchange?
Let's start that change.

Avril Chester

Avril - Change can mean so many different things – you changing, others changing, the world around you changing. I'd like to introduce our second book sponsor Mark Lockton-Goddard, CEO of embracent. I absolutely knew this chapter was perfect for Mark, not only because of the name but because of everything Mark supports and does.

Mark - I spent many years as a CIO, and in consulting, and then decided to set up my own business, which, I'm not sure whether that was sensible or foolhardy. It was one of those two. I wanted to create a consultancy business that was much more sensible, pragmatic and experience based – one that I would like to work for.

We are now coming up to five years and it's been the most enjoyable, the most challenging, and the most interesting five years that I've had for a long time.

The first thing to note is that starting a business, and then running and leading it through a pandemic is certainly very different to anything I had done before. When I worked as a CIO for some very large global organisations, I had a team of staff I could manage but now I've had to try to become more of a leader, and of course there is a big difference.

We've had to create a brand, an ethos, decide what is important to us and get everyone brought into that vision. There's a great phrase: 'You're only a leader of people if they are prepared to follow.' And in my experience, people want to follow a purpose that matters rather than just make a big salary.

It's also been interesting to take the shackles off myself. Being in corporate life for 25 years, I didn't realise that I had become slightly limited in what I could and couldn't do. After some months of running my own business, I suddenly thought, hang on, I can actually go and do 'that' if I want to, nobody's going to stop me.

That was a real Eureka moment for me, because I think in corporate life, without even noticing it I was slightly blinkered to what was possible. Suddenly, everything was possible. But on the flip side of that, lots of things were not really possible, because we didn't have the money and/or the people to do everything we wanted to. So, I was constantly playing this game of what I'd like to do with what I was able to do.

It's been a huge change.

Avril - For someone that's thinking about changing careers perhaps even thinking about starting their own business, what nugget of advice would you offer them Mark?

Mark - I would say business is all about telling stories and understanding what stories people want to listen to. It's got to resonate. You have to really listen very carefully to people – to understand the theme and tone of what's important to them. And then think carefully about how you tell your story to bring people with you.

I spent the first six months trying to manage my way into a business. And then I realised it wasn't about just managing tasks, you have to have a purpose, you have to have a vision. And that has to come from what's inside you and what's inside the people you work with.

Avril - Having gone through personal change in terms of moving from a CIO into a different kind of leader and shaping an organisation. Mark has created a company that is centred around change, but I must, just must, ask about the company name.

Mark - We kicked around different names at the start of the company, as you do. And there was a lot of talk about technology at the time being disruptive, and technology affecting people's lives. I got the sense that a lot of the press at the time and the sentiments were all a bit negative. Technology is going to put people out of work, it's going to challenge them, it's going to change them, it's going to be difficult.

And I thought well, yes, it can be all of those things, but technology is like any tool, ultimately it can be used for good or for bad, depending on who's holding the trigger.

So I thought, where's the positive because there are so many great aspects around technology, so many great ways that you can use technology for good. Technology is creating new ways of working all the time. From being able to spot early signs of cancer on images or being able to understand people's behaviours and emotions from instant messages.

Technology is being used all the time to allow us to do things that we never thought possible. So why do we focus on the negatives? Why is it all doom and gloom?

When building this company I wanted to make sure that we were focused on positively embracing technology for good. Our name comes from embrace new technology 'embracent'.

There's also a play on that as well in that 'NT' always stood for new technology. But it was also new thinking, new teams, new times. Embrace lots of different positive meanings. The best technology of today will be outdated tomorrow. It was more about being open in your mindset to embrace things that come to you, rather than be disrupted by them. And the new technology, of course, we are a technology business. But it's not just about technology. It's about thinking. It's about people.

Avril - I didn't know that about the 'NT', super clever Mark, I love it. Let's touch on new technology and the future. What are you seeing now that really excites you?

Mark - A lot of the companies that we work for make bad decisions around technology. They don't understand what is really possible, they don't understand how to organise themselves to take advantage of it. They make poor decisions, the governance is wrong, and some struggle to fund it properly, do the change management and really embrace the technology.

What we are focused on at embracent is simple technology done well. Let's get the basics right otherwise people end up working and doing their jobs, in spite of the technology, not with the technology.

And the other thing is scale, you have the availability of thinking power. You can scale up now in a way that you can never do. For example if you previously wanted to analyse all the UK data on climate change, for example, it would have taken years, and it would have been incredibly expensive.

Now you just spin up a bunch of AWS services, you spin up a bunch of different capabilities. You spin up things. What's fascinating for me is the fact that you can scale so quickly. I'll give you an example, we wanted to create a new customer survey so that everything we do is backed by an understanding of whether we did a good job or not? And we decided to incorporate sentiment analysis, an AI that helps us understand not just what people are saying, but what's behind what they're saying, based on the words that they choose, and the order.

And all this is now possible by simply buying a sentiment analysis tool off Google for a few dollars. You couldn't do that previously; you'd probably have to spend a lot of money with someone like IBM to build something for you. So, the tools you need you can just buy as a service and consume it. Then pull it all together and do something incredible. It's not a case of you having to invent it, you just essentially go and subscribe to a service. And I find that so exciting because it's putting power, massive power into even the smallest businesses hands.

Avril - This book is about the positive impact of technology and the wonderful stories you may not have heard about. Mark is a great supporter of hospices. Precious places at a very difficult time at the end of life. I'm keen to learn more about your work, Mark.

Mark - I have supported hospices for 15 years, since both my parents sadly passed away because of cancer. When my father was in Bolton Hospice, in the hands of some wonderful people, I was struck by how incredible those people were, and the amazing jobs they do.

And the fact that they didn't just care about my parents, but they cared about me, my brother, my sister, they cared about everything and everybody to a level that you just wouldn't imagine.

I was also struck by how poorly supported they were. They were functioning with very little technology support, without any proper funding, having to raise their own funds, having to use old technology and manual bits of paper. They were making such a massive difference with hardly any of the tools that you would expect of even a small business these days.

I've now worked with a range of different hospices – giving advice on technology strategy – and I'm also the chair of HQP, a charity that supports many hospices up and down the country as a buying group. It's a simple model to help hospices join together to get the best possible price on key products and services.

My company embracent is on a HQP framework for providing digital technology skills and experience to hospices at a heavily discounted price, or sometimes a pro bono price, because those organisations should have access to the best technology out there. They are underfunded, they're struggling, they need to maximise every dollar. What we do is help them in a range of different ways, in a way that they can consume. Because they are often small businesses, they don't even understand technology, they might not even have a technology manager.

It's about giving them better tools, it's about giving them better automations of manual processes, understanding their data and how can they better serve their patients. It's about helping them embrace technology so that they care for more people, more of the time.

Avril - Mark ran the London Marathon in 2010, amazing. I used to love running long distance at school, but I'm not quite sure what happened. What can we learn from putting ourselves through something like a marathon? What nugget of wisdom does Mark have for us from treading the streets of London and completing those 26 miles and 385 yards.

Mark - Don't shake everybody's hand as you're going along because it slows you down!

But seriously, when I started I couldn't even run to the corner. I learned that you can do things that you can't imagine if you really are focused and dedicated and work hard. I trained for nine months and got to the point where I could run a marathon. I never thought I could do that and it was a real eye opener to me about what people are capable of when they allow themselves to embrace new possibilities.

At the start I thought, I'll never be able to do this. But for me it was a challenge and a focus. I felt like I needed to run the marathon – to raise money for hospices and to thank the people at Bolton Hospice for the dedication they had shown to my father. And therefore I wanted to be true to that vision. And I wanted to stick to that. You can do things that surprise yourself.

Avril - Thank you so much, Mark. We can actively change. Similarly, change is sometimes forced upon us. What nuggets of advice are there for us?

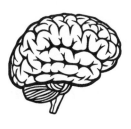

Let's share wisdom!

"Be the change you want to see in the world then we will create a world founded on inclusion, a world where we leave no one behind."

Dr Jacqui Taylor
CEO and Co-founder of FlyingBinary and #15 most
influential UK technologist

"If it doesn't challenge you, it doesn't change you. Your comfort zone is a beautiful place, but nothing ever grows there."

Beth Younger
Process Lead at embracent

"If someone were to come into your workplace and replace you, what would they do that is different or better? Then why are you not doing those things?"

Eileen Jennings-Brown
Top 50 Most Influential Women in the UK Tech.
Head of Technology for the Wellcome Trust

"Don't fear change. Be proud of the past, and be brave about the future."

Freddie Quek
CTO Times Higher Education, passionate about
addressing Digital Inclusion for all by #JoiningtheDots

*"If we all make small intentional
changes, they are the catalyst
for the positive impact we want
others to experience."*

Serena Walker
Marketing Strategist, Trustee, Speaker, Mentor

*"Change starts with you,
open your mind to the
opportunities it can bring."*

Amanda Khan
Head of Change Delivery at the RIBA

*"You will only be successful with
your Digital / IT transformation
if your organisational culture
and leadership has a mindset for
continual adaptation and change."*

Dr Kuldip S Sandhu
CIO / IT Director & Management Consultant

*"It is often only once we have planned our
route, that Purpose taps us on the shoulder
and leads us towards our destiny – learn to
recognise it and welcome it as a friend."*

Simon Nelson
Police Leader and Disability Champion,
Board Advisor to Cancer Central

Avril - Purpose certainly tapped me on the shoulder, an unexpected change in my life which in turn led me to meet wonderful new people such as you, Simon. I am absolutely loving these nuggets. Steven, it is really fulfilling asking for advice and support in the form of nuggets. Thank you for starting this and your idea for this book. I hope you have been highlighting, sticking notes and scribbling down the sides.

Before we move on, I wish to stop and thank everyone who has contributed to this book. I was extremely nervous asking each of you. Reaching out to my network to ask for support and help, with the incredible generosity already shown with Cancer Central I was worried I was pushing this ask just that step too far. Your kindness in sharing your wisdom with others and allowing me to publish as a fundraiser for Cancer Central means the world. I'm learning an incredible amount from you all too. Thank you.

Right, tea or wine stop? Don't take too long, we're thriving here.

Chapter 6
Thrive

To share
Is a scare
Yet more minds
Shapes new finds

Avril Chester

Avril - Now we're cooking (tick, next food reference), sorry I can't help it. We've reflected on life, invented, eaten, given ourselves a boost and embraced change. Therefore, it's time to thrive. I find to thrive, I need to involve others, share my ideas, learn what's wrong with them and find a way through. Linda and her potatoes have done just that. Let's hear her favourite quote and her story.

"Everything in life depends on
how that life accepts its limits."

James Baldwin

Linda - This speaks to my soul. I didn't accept limits when NatureWrap Foodtech was received with doubt "potatoes, really?", or when firms and industry bodies purporting to be concerned with innovation in food systems (and food waste) weren't, or dealing with the barriers female and under-represented entrepreneurs face in the business world so were unable to fulfil their mandate to provide market access in any tangible way beyond sound bites of 'empowerment'.

Taking inventory of my business development skills and the fortitude to deliver when undermined, my business partners asked me to devise and implement the market entry strategy. I ignored all the armchair business experts. The plan has resulted in a great reception by the UK potato processing market (and other target markets). We have engaged clients who wish to integrate NatureWrap's food preservation technology process into their production line.

What is it about potatoes?

The dominant industry preservative, sodium metabisulphite (SMBS) limits growth in the fresh preserved potato sector because of short shelf life and odour problems which has discouraged processors to develop product lines. "UK food service sector waste was estimated at £3.2 billion/year in 2018" – 40% of that included potato that ends up in landfills.

The potato processing sector is a multi-billion-dollar industry and potato is said to be the fourth most consumed crop in the world.

I think there is something rather comforting and wholesome about potatoes. Who remembers the student days of running out of money and the delight of finding a few pound coins at the back of the sofa and dashing off to the fish and chip shop?

The comforting feeling of tucking into chunky cut chips soaked with vinegar along the Pier in Brighton while being lashed by wind and rain, suddenly the harshness of the elements seems bearable?

How about the hero's welcome you receive after the victorious negotiations with the chef just before the bar kitchen closes means your table can enjoy some chips with the beverage of choice? Or the fuss at Christmas about whose potato salad or roast potatoes are the best? Of course, mine win every time! I won't hear any different. Masterchef... hello!

NatureWrap food technology preserves fresh cut potatoes by more than five times the industry average, uses only natural, plant-based, no SMBS, non-allergenic preservatives. Covid-19 and Brexit reinforced the urgent need of robust local food supply chains. 'Just in Time' days are passed.

What happened in your trip up North?

Whilst there is never ending talk of supporting innovation in foodtech / agritech, all of the events that were organised by the various firms were held in London. Any 'meet the buyer - farm to fork' events were focused nearer the fork end. Considerable government and private sector research funding is currently applied to primary agricultural challenges and improving farming methods or food apps, food delivery etc. NatureWrap falls into the mid-stream; post-harvest food preservation and waste reduction technology, we have therefore had no access to the public funding.

After launching in the UK in early 2019 we weren't making the level of progress I desired. I hear madness is doing the same thing and hoping for a different outcome so I ignored all the London events and expert advice, and hatched a plan to go to the UK potato-processing region and speak to potential clients directly. Our Chairman had a bemused look when I announced that he should accompany me to the potato fair in Harrogate, Yorkshire.

"Have you ever been to Harrogate? Have you seen the flood warnings, the area is being battered by storms?" My response was "No and yes, but the show must go on". I showed him the list of the companies we were to speak with and explained the route to market. He and our chief scientist saw the method in my madness.

Undeterred by the November howling wind and rain, we (our chief scientist dodged the drip on account of living in Australia) boarded our train from London Kings Cross to Harrogate and its potato conference where we finally met our target market.

Suddenly, the usual blank stares at unfocused events were replaced with looks of intrigue followed by "tell me more", "how can we work together?", "when can we have a follow up meeting?". Our innovation was well received by our target market who we are now working with.

What is the social impact of NatureWrap?

Sustainable Impact: Economic, Social and Environmental.

Additional employment and opportunities.

Achieving our target of building a new market sector where long shelf life, sulphur-free fresh potatoes and other vegetables are available will create direct and indirect jobs in farming, processing and distribution in the UK (and other target markets) and increase sector productivity. In collaboration with our food processing partners, we will create new jobs in product transportation, distribution, retail, and other services. The over five times increase in shelf life is instrumental in achieving the above as well as new export opportunities. The potential impact on our partners' gross revenue in the UK and worldwide is significant.

Food opportunities

The application provides options for shelf life extension for fried, mashed, boiled or roasted potatoes.

Waste Reduction, Circular Economy and Power Generation

More than 20,000 trucks travel to the UK every year, importing 700,000 tonnes of processed potato products (World Potato Markets, 'Brexit and the Potato Industry, 2018'). Developing a local market will reduce the CO_2 emissions and road congestion.

Diversity of thought

Our intergenerational team of scientists, engineers and a female CEO exemplify diversity and the solutions that STEM and business can produce.

Where do you see the future of the potato?

I see endless possibilities for the humble potato, a dynamic vegetable that can be used in multiple dishes and demand continues to rise due to the increase in plant-based diets.

The waste can be used to generate power via anaerobic plant digestors as well as in bioplastics for use in fashion eye wear, furniture and packaging, who knew?! On a few occasions at conferences I've heard warm utterings of "Ohhh, you are the potato lady, I've heard about you.". We can toast to all this with potato vodka cocktails, why not?

Linda Achan
Co-founder and CEO, NatureWrap UK and EnergyWells LLC

Avril - Potato vodka cocktails, Linda? You're on.

'People are busy. Don't confuse that with unwilling.' Unsure about asking for help, let Catherine Ann guide you.

Catherine Ann - Rare Disease Day is held each year on the last day of February to raise awareness of rare diseases, help understanding and improve access to medical representation.

My daughter Chloe has Cohen Syndrome, a rare autosomal recessive genetic condition that, for her, presents itself as severe learning difficulties, retinitis pigmentosa, gross and fine motor skill challenges, hypotonia, microcephaly and curvature of the spine... she's also very funny, incredibly charming, and the most stoic person I know.

Having Chloe changed many things for me including my career path. If you don't already know, she's the inspiration behind doqit. I was having my coffee this morning, giving gratitude for my girl, and I wanted to share why a rare child is a blessing, not a hinderance, and what Chloe has taught me on my journey to being a better entrepreneur.

How do you eat an elephant?

The red book, nursery, paediatrician – it all felt very target driven. Sitting up, stacking bricks, walking. Chloe was smiling, she was happy; but I knew we had targets. I wanted her to achieve a target, and I wanted her to want to achieve a target. But how...? The same way you eat an elephant – one bit at a time. We never stopped focusing on the end goal and we got there by breaking every task into small component parts; like stacking bricks – recognise the bricks are there, touch a brick, pick it up, and always...

celebrate small wins.

Celebrating small wins helps keep your eye on the prize and safe in the knowledge that the end goal is in sight. Encouragement, loud cheering and whooping over the years has kept momentum going and belief that: 'Well, if we've done that, we can do this!' However, sometimes things don't go to plan, so...

if it doesn't work, try a new way.

Just because it's worked for someone else, and it's documented as the 'best' way, doesn't mean it will work for you. Having a long career in sales, I know the value of flogging a dead horse – nil!

Going back to the bricks, one of the reasons Chloe couldn't stack the bricks was because she couldn't see them. I can hear that penny drop! Sometimes, it's not until years later that the reason something hasn't worked is uncovered – Chloe was about ten before we knew she had little sight. Thank goodness we didn't wait to try new ways until then. But all of this takes...

patience.

In the words of Gary Barlow, sometimes we 'just need to have a little patience'. Patience is hard. We live in a world where everything is now, disposable, and so little joy. Chloe's condition has demanded patience, and this has taught me that this much-needed time of reflection brings joy and a depth of understanding of what has been achieved, and what has to be done next. Like any journey though, we needed to...

listen to the experts.

There's never been so much available knowledge as there is today; and there will be more tomorrow, and the day after. I remember asking Chloe's geneticist why he'd chosen that area of medicine. He believes that in his lifetime it's the area where most progress will be made and is now part of the 100,000 Genomes Project at Oxford University – mind blowing. How lucky we are to have so many dedicated experts around us. People who take a strand of expertise and make it their life's work, who are willing to share their knowledge and time. All we have to do is...

ask for help.

People are busy. Don't confuse that with unwilling. People are generally very kind and want to help. Know your limits. Having children – with or without a condition – is exhausting. The juggle of life, work, school is overwhelming. So don't try and do it all yourself and be a martyr to the midnight oil, just ask. And, finally....

NEVER GIVE UP!

I'm not talking about flogging the dead horse, I'm talking about being fearless in your quest to know more, learning from the research, embracing the experts, rallying the supporters and knowing that the prize your eye's on is there for the taking.

So, thank you my darling Chloe for helping me on my journey to being the best I can be, for teaching me more than I could ever have hoped to learn and making me proud every day.

Catherine Ann Reid
CEO Doqit. Passionate about making a positive
contribution to the wellbeing of people and the planet

Avril - Chloe, thanks for showing us how to thrive every day. Gary Barlow, you've made it twice into this book, does that mean we can get your autograph now? You know people keep telling me I need a famous ambassador or patron for Cancer Central (hint, does anyone know Gary Barlow?)... OK, back to reality. It's easy to get carried away and at times, be our worst enemy. Su has some experience to share...

"Your deadline is an important tool, but not mandatory."

Su - The thinking behind this nugget came from a growing realisation that while deadlines (and with this I include targets, measurements and other methods of holding ourselves and others to account) are superb tools for making things happen, they can also be counterproductive, unduly stressful and take us down the wrong path. Let me explain ...

Before the pandemic I'm not sure many of us appreciated or achieved that elusive work/life balance. It became clearer when we were all forced to press the pause button and family came more into focus. Priorities and deadlines changed – never truer than when we, or someone we love, faced illness. In these circumstances, work deadlines became irrelevant.

A deadline (or target) is only useful in the right context. If the context changes, change or even remove the deadline.

But deadlines are still important tools in the right context. Without them, our days can be disorganised, directionless and lack progress.

The issue comes when we set unrealistic or incorrect deadlines and do what others are doing rather than what is right for us.

Sometimes hitting the pause button to re-evaluate a deadline or target can be the best decision ever.

I'll give you an example from my personal life.

A number of years ago, a friend recommended a meditation app and I thought I'd give it a go. I learnt the basics while experimenting with time of day and how long I could sit without being uninterrupted by family or work.

I was horrified to realise that at first I couldn't find three minutes of unterrupted time in my day. Eventually I settled on starting first thing in the morning, when I was least likely to be interrupted, and started to eke out a regular 10 minutes a day. I realised that if I didn't meditate before work in the morning, I never found time during the rest of the day – my deadline was meditate by 8am, or forget it…

Except at the weekends!

Su Copeland
Marketing for Scientists and Engineers

Avril - Yay Su, ringfencing weekends, it's super important to hit pause. My pause button and treat is a cup of tea in bed. Something so small, but somehow it feels so luxurious. I'd like to take a moment to reflect on how technology has changed our working lives, in particular allowing our lives to thrive.

Ryan - People and technology work best together, but you need to know how to get the best out of your tools.

Throughout my career I've benefitted from using technology to support my work and lifestyle. I'm happiest working on a results basis and having great software and hardware tools can make that a reality.

For the last 15 months I've worked as a digital nomad – I've taken my family back to South Africa for close on 15 months. We've based ourselves in Johannesburg and have made the effort to travel to various spots across South Africa. I've been able to do this whilst working remotely.

I've leveraged a good internet connection, stable and sturdy hardware with a good set of headphones. I've needed to learn how to juggle the travel with parental duties and finding a spot to do a call.

It has meant that my young kids have had their dad nearby, they've been able to spend time with their grandparents, they have memories of some of the most beautiful places in the world and they have learnt about their homeland.

Ryan Purvis
My passion is transforming business to leverage
digital technology and tools

Avril - So pleased to hear all is going well in South Africa, Ryan. I know so many of us have thought about moving or moved over recent years. Really exhilarating and, yes, I may have spent many an hour or two dreaming on Rightmove. Perhaps it is time to apologise to my partner and parents for sending endless new home links? Hmmm… let's swiftly move on. To thrive we also need to let go of our fears, but how do we do that?

Reema - Having worked with leaders globally for 20 years, previously as VP/MD for a Silicon Valley business and a Founder and CEO, I have seen some leaders navigate fear and failure for exponential success, and others suppress their fears to the point of mental disorders, addictions, and gradual death.

As an executive and high-performance coach for senior leaders and entrepreneurs, some people are surprised to hear those successful leaders, the ones who appear to have it all, also have a need to challenge and navigate their deepest fears to create exponential success.

From the hundreds of high performing leaders I've coached, what is clear is that for leaders to create a successful step up to the next level, it's their conscious and unconscious fears that they need to get past to achieve the fulfilment and success they deeply desire.

Fear shows up as limiting beliefs and behaviours. From judgements and biases, procrastination of day-to-day tasks, to the need for perfection and control, or an excuse for countless distractions.

None of these are healthy, yet many people do not realise that these are symptoms and not the root cause of fear that's built up over years of conscious and unconscious learned responses, beliefs, and behaviours.

Avoiding fear is common. Humans are wired to use the signal of fear to keep safe, instead of risking death by standing out instead of fitting in.

Most of us are taught how to protect ourselves earlier on in our lives. From what we should or should not do, say, or touch, and how we should fit in based on societal norms, in school and at work.

In the workplace I commonly see people blocked with these three reactions:

I'm scared of

- People: What will others think or say? If I fail or start something and then don't finish it.

- Time and Energy: I'm afraid if I do too much it will take over my life/make me a bad person/tire me out.

- Money: I'm afraid I'll lose my job, lose clients, my lifestyle and be less well off. Or if I make too much money then what will others think, say or do?

I don't know what to do
(This usually comes from a place of 'I don't have enough')

- Information. I don't know where to start / I'm overwhelmed by the options.

- Skills: I don't know what to do and how to do it.

- Connections: I don't know whom to ask. I find it hard to ask for what I really want.

- Motivation to leave my comfort zone: It's easier to stay where I am even if I am unhappy because I need money for a bigger house.

I'm not good enough

- To believe in myself enough: who am I? Why would they listen to me? And, again, what would others think if...?

- To be accepted: I fear rejection and hearing the word no.

So, how do successful leaders navigate fear effectively? For me, the answers are rooted in psychology and neuroscience.

Dr Carol Dweck's Growth Mindset and Emotional Intelligence, popularised by Professor Daniel Goleman, support the notion that self-awareness and self-regulation of one's thoughts and emotions to respond and act effectively are key to cultivating positive behaviours and outcomes.

Here are five behaviours and traits that I see leaders who are more fulfilled in their success when managing their fears:

1. They replace their judgements with openness and curiosity. They do this by having an ability to be more present and aware of their own thoughts.

2. They get good at failing by looking at it through the lens of learning and they keep building that muscle by 'failing forward'.

3. They can self-regulate their emotions by letting go of what they can't control and put boundaries in place around what they can control.

4. Servant Leadership: They carry out their work from a place of serving and empowering others rather than putting themselves first.

5. They learn to view their vulnerability as a strength and have the courage to take risks on initiatives they are passionate about. Which allows them to lead with greater purpose and authenticity.

The next time you experience emotions of fear, ask yourself what's the real desire I have that I'm resisting because of fear? Which of the five steps above could it be helpful for me to explore in relation to that? And if I do what possibilities could that open for me?

Reema Gainley
Founder and Executive Coach at Lead
from Within www.reemagainley.com

Avril - I've just ran out of my highlighter pen. Reema you are a superstar, thank you. Be gone, fear! This reminds me of one of my favourite quotes which accompanied me during some pretty dark times (namely chemo): "Courage doesn't mean you don't get afraid. Courage means you don't let fear stop you." - Bethany Hamilton.

It's time to stand up, shake around and sit back down again. Go on, I dare you. Seriously, how many of you have just read on without a little invigoration of the body? Hmmm...

We're thriving, we're buzzing and we're going to close this last story chapter with a big fat YES!

Tiffany - Can technology change lives; make a difference – can that be true? Could it be that working in technology, you could have a material impact on someone's life? My answer is: 'Yes, you can!'

I have been privileged to work for many organisations that have implemented many life-changing technologies. From connecting people through Africa and across the world, to helping people see and hear, and now to supporting people through dying, death or bereavement.

Technology is an intrinsic part of life whether we like it or not. You can hear the collective groan when the internet stops working in the office (or home office!), or feel that frustration when you can't open your banking app to transfer that cash. Obsessively checking how many steps you've done or what the quality of your sleep was the night before. Technology gives us never-ending access to anything, anywhere and at any time we want it.

And yes, it can be a daunting thought, but technology is a beautiful addition to our daily lives – facilitating conversations across the globe where you feel like you are in the same room, sharing that glass of wine with a long-distance friend from years back.

What I love is that to many, this all happens by magic. The internet is just there, the person just pops up on the screen and your precious pennies are visible in just one click.

The reality is that there is an army of IT warriors who dedicate their lives to this magic. From writing lines and lines of complex code to provide a simple interface for you to talk to your loved ones, to working tirelessly to connect miles and miles of cables, even underwater cables, so that you can binge the latest series on Netflix.

Then there is the more sobering side of technology. In the same way those cables carry data for streaming your favourite show, they carry precious data about our health, our money, our lives, facilitating the sharing of information so that at your time of need, our medical teams can help you. Surgeons are now using technology to assist them when operating and medical devices that can save lives. And even at the end of life, we are supported though the use of technology.

It is an honour to be a part of this army of brilliant, fascinating, intelligent, and cool people and to make such a difference to our world.

Tiffany Willcox
Chief Technology Officer, Marie Curie

Avril - Tiffany, I adore your nugget: 'Yes, you can!' Super powerful. I also wish to thank you and everyone at Marie Curie for all the incredible work you do at a very challenging time. Our time is precious so let's thrive with our nuggets.

Let's share
wisdom!

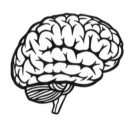

*"Never sweat the small stuff,
except when small incremental
improvements are all that stand
between you and success."*

Graeme K Hackland
25 Year Formula 1 IT Professional

*"Be curious. How will you ever find
your passion if you stay within the
confines of your comfort zone?"*

Caroline Carruthers
Author, Chief Executive, Data Cheerleader

"Always go into things with an open mind, expectations screw you up."

Alison Davis
Passionate about IT Leadership and Rugby

"Just remember there is no sure fire way to win. If you don't play it's guaranteed that you never will."

Ezechi Britton MBE
From Developer to Co-Founder and CTO,
to Serial Entrepreneur and VC. It's been quite a journey!

"This has been my mantra for years. To quote Tony Robbins: 'It is in your moments of decision that your destiny is shaped.'"

Vinay Sonchatla
Live life like there is no tomorrow

"Make sure your career is something you love. You'll spend a long time doing it so choose a career that makes you happy."

Declan Hunt
Technology and Digital professional who specialises in supporting organisations through significant transformational change. Following a career as a successful CIO in organisations such as Macmillan Cancer Support and G4S, he is now a freelance consultant specialising in digital and technology transformation. Declan is also a Trustee of the London Irish Centre.

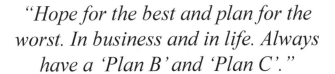

"Learning to effectively manage expectations is a key stepping stone to success."

Daniel Warburton
Co-Founder CIO Watercooler, where IT leaders share ideas

"Hope for the best and plan for the worst. In business and in life. Always have a 'Plan B' and 'Plan C'."

Jon Downing
Property and Business Investor. Mentor to ambitious entrepreneurs, Board Advisor to Cancer Central

· 127 ·

"A formula for success or failure:
Opportunity + Response = Fortune

Learn to identify opportunities in all areas of life

How you choose to respond to those opportunities is
critical – ignore them or let them slip by and they're
gone; act on opportunities in a positive and engaging
way and you've got a fighting chance of success

How you notice opportunities (or not) and how you
respond to them (or don't) will determine your
fortune (good or bad).

Like any authentic habit that you develop, this formula
becomes easier and more consistent over time."

Greg Morley
Happy soul having a human experience and CIO

Avril - It is our responsibility to help others thrive around us if we want to be a fully inclusive society. Julia Smith, D&I writer, women's and LGBTQIA+ rights activist, and a data-driven marketer beautifully wrote: "Team leaders and business owners must learn to appreciate their workforce for what they do whilst fully respecting their autonomy – the fact that people can be different from you: different life paths, different bodies, different needs and aspirations. Ideals in workplace are always unrealistic – they are always ableist, crude and cruel. Only via a compassionate and kind outlook to life, one can enrich and celebrate a collective of individuals, rather than merely tolerate an individual collective."

Chapter 7
Inclusion

*All should
be included,
With no-one
excluded.*

Avril Chester

Avril - The technology and digital divide was laid bare by the pandemic, but so too were the incredible initiatives that sprang into action to address this. A hero of mine in this space is Freddie.

#JoiningtheDots - Be the Change. Our Personal Social Responsibility.

Freddie - When Covid started the UK's lockdown in March 2020, the things that the technology profession took for granted became a nightmare for others and technology leaders became 'heroes' by switching to remote working to achieve business continuity. But it also revealed the scale of digital poverty in exposing the damage to education and society that austerity and digital exclusion have created.

This is the story of how the UK's technology leaders' communities came together as one strong community voice to inject digital poverty policy and debate into the country's social and political agenda, challenging each of us to consider our social responsibility to do something that is in our domain.

Digital Exclusion and why should we care?

The lockdown had a greater effect on people who are digitally excluded. According to Ofcom, six per cent of households and 18% of over-64s do not have home internet access; 20% of children do not have a suitable device for their home schooling. Whether the pandemic ends or continues tomorrow, it has especially affected those who live in socially disadvantaged households whose day-to-day reality is having no digital connection – phones, apps, social media or the internet. They cannot have remote lessons or do their schoolwork. They are effectively being left behind.

As a father with two children, I witnessed first-hand how they coped with remote learning, the need for their own computers, workspace and a reliable home broadband connection. The UK is the world's fifth largest economy, so how can this be? At the start of 2021 I spoke with 60+ leaders over six weeks across nine communities representing 90,000 tech professionals and many, like me, were not fully aware of the digital poverty landscape. They wanted to help but it was difficult to know how to, although it was heart-warming to know that there are more than 70 device donation initiatives out there, including a celebrity-led campaign by David Beckham and David Walliams that raised £10.6m in three weeks, big companies like Asda and Dell donating 7,000 laptops, and Amazon donating 10,000 tablets. However, if we think we have made a dent in solving this problem, then we are completely mistaken. The gaps are still huge and many of these initiatives are tactical, not scalable or sustainable. We need to go beyond starting from the same obvious place and thinking it is about having a device.

Joined-up thinking and action

We have to join up the provision of digital access, which includes devices, data, support, skills, opportunity, cybersafe practices, appropriate content and user experience. I was overwhelmed by the collective desire across the tech leaders' communities to address digital exclusion together:

UK IT Leaders (Dave Jones), S.E.E.D. (Shakeeb Niazi), Horizon CIO Network (Mark Chillingworth), HotTopics.ht (Philip Randerson), CIO WaterCooler (Daniel Warburton), BCS, The Chartered Institute for IT (John Higgins), Tech Monitor (Cristina Lago), Computing (John Leonard), Charity IT Leaders (Tree Hall), CIO Online (Doug Drinkwater), IDC (Marc Dowd/Chris Weston), Tech London Advocates & Global Tech Advocates (Russ Shaw), Digital Leaders (Robin Knowles).

#JoiningtheDots, as the name suggests, realises that there are lots of good initiatives and if they are joined up then the impact will be far greater. Together we can go further and faster by socialising and mobilising its combined 130,000 members, and the rest of the country.

Digital Poverty Alliance

There is now a realisation that digital poverty goes beyond the nation's schoolchildren. It also includes the elderly who have not been exposed to the digital world, or those who have no means to access it.

As the pandemic revealed, digital touches each and every one of these issues. Chillingworth, Founder of Horizon CIO Network wrote in his article: "Digital poverty has to be dealt with. The UK faces a skills shortage and a productivity issue. If sections of society are digitally excluded this will only exacerbate these problems and therefore increase other national issues... which reduce competitiveness and, taken from a business lens, reduce profitability and innovation."

One of the missing pieces of this complex jigsaw puzzle was the lack of a framework that enabled government departments, corporations, professional bodies, grassroots communities and individuals to be joined up. Then one day came a chat with Paul Finnis, CEO of Learning Foundation who shared his plans for creating the Digital Poverty Alliance, co-founded with the Institution of Engineering and Technology with backing from Currys. Launched in October 2021, it aims to end digital exclusion by 2030. Co-chair Lord Jim Knight, a former education minister, explains: "Governments can only do so much… There are still 10 million people that are not online… (it requires) a collective rethink on how we face globalisation, technology change, climate change, migration and conflict."

The #JoiningtheDots community of 13 UK Tech Leaders communities has become a Community Board Member, with many technology leaders becoming its Ambassadors.

Be the Change

This pandemic has made me rethink and realise if I can just do something small to help anyone, one person at a time, and if others share the same thinking, then we can create a collective impact that is far greater. It starts with each of us taking that step as our personal social responsibility, and mine is to help socialise and signpost what we know about digital inclusion initiatives so that we can mobilise those who want to help in a more strategic and focused way. The British Computer Society (BCS) whose purpose is "Making IT Good for Society", has made addressing digital divide as one of its strategic priorities. As Chair of its newly established Digital Divide Specialist Group, I now have the opportunity to mobilise its 60,000 members to this cause.

As technology professionals, we are in a privileged position as we have been dealing with technological changes and disruptions throughout our careers. Who else is better placed to have the opportunity and expertise to do something about this? Let's all start with one person, thing, or action at a time. Make it our personal social responsibility. Be the Change by #JoiningtheDots.

Freddie Quek
CTO Times Higher Education, passionate about addressing Digital Inclusion for all by #JoiningtheDots

Avril - 'Be the change', this is exactly what Serena did.

Serena - Technology is so prevalent there is hardly any part of our lives in which it has no impact. Technology has evolved over many years but the rate of acceleration in recent years has been phenomenal, and we now have a whole generation, Generation Alpha, who are truly digital natives. Most technology benefits us as citizens and consumers and, whatever our view, it is increasingly essential in many aspects of our lives.

I have been lucky to have seen this evolution and the impact it has had on how we live our lives. I have also seen how so many different people and skills come together to create many of the technology solutions we use. Many ideas come from inside the technology industry, but just as many come from outside and are turned into reality by technologists. These ideas prove that good ideas can be turned into reality if the right people are brought together and the vision is good.

Many years ago, the chair of a regatta, wanted the yachtsmen to have access to the Internet to print their scores and other details without leaving the quay. They needed a solution. The CEO of the technology company I worked for at the time gave the project to me, and I had to provide a solution that achieved the goal.

Why was I set the challenge? I had never worked on a project like this and I'm in marketing! However, I said yes and gathered a team together! I had no idea if it was possible but having said yes, we had to deliver and deliver we did. We pulled together, designed, and built the infrastructure and delivered a solution back to the chair and it worked! The ripple effect of a success project was felt by everyone involved directly or indirectly. Without all the diversity of skills, the different approaches, and thought processes, it would have been even more of a challenge to have succeeded.

There are many stories of ideas being transformed into reality by a diversely skilled team. That is what inspires me and has empowered me throughout my career to reach further, to push myself and to keep sharing ideas knowing that, even if I can't create the code, there is somebody somewhere who can.

We all use technology in some way, shape or form. Technology allows us to communicate across the globe, to reach our families through voice, text and video. We are digitally connected in a way that we could not have imagined even 50 years ago.

Imagine how 2020/21 would have played out even 30 years ago. So many of us benefitted from our ability to communicate, to see those we work with and those we love regularly aided by technology.

But not all of us were so fortunate. This set off a train of thought and I asked myself whether we are doing all we can to help those with visual or hearing impairment? Are we using all the tools available to include everyone? It takes conscious consideration and deliberate action to ensure that our technology is inclusive of as many people as possible.

We all use technology daily and the pace of change is increasing. There have been great steps in making technology more inclusive, with accessibility software available on many platforms for businesses, schools, and charities but we need to extend the reach of these capabilities even further.

We need to continually ask ourselves: 'Is this technology truly inclusive?' And answer honestly. Too often minority groups can be missed. We must change our approach, so we ensure the changes we need are made and our technology is as inclusive as possible.

The positive impact of technology is undoubted and far reaching. There is a strong connection between science, technology, engineering and maths (STEM), a fusion that works harmoniously to develop solutions as diverse as robotic surgery, nano-level measurement, automated warehousing and delivery and collection and analysis of data for performance analysis of athletes. Diverse teams spread around the globe routinely collaborate to create many and varied solutions. I am fortunate to have been a part of this.

I am passionate about inspiring the next generation of STEM talent to realise their dreams. Representation matters and being a female from an ethnic group in the UK in the tech sector makes a difference to those who don't or hardly see anyone that looks like them. We can all be part of building a better place for future generations. All of our actions can create change, even the smallest positive action creates a ripple effect that spreads and enables wider inclusion. The more diverse the creators, the more positive the technology will be.

Make a small change today. Make it an intentional change, and it impacts the future.

Serena Walker
Marketing Strategist, Trustee, Speaker, Mentor

Avril - Inclusion is for all, as Freddie and Stephen back in our chapter called 'Invent' mention, we mustn't forget to support every generation.

Dominic - With the advancement of technology over time there often seems to be a generational separation between the old and the young – 'It wasn't like that in my day.', 'You wouldn't understand if I explained it to you.' and such-like; a separation of those who have and those who have not.

A few years ago, I was very lucky to take part in a sponsored digital inclusion initiative in partnership with one of our clients. This simply involved all staff members across the country taking working time off to visit their local care homes with laptops / iPads and speaking with the residents. I was lucky enough to visit a local care home in Maidstone, equipped only with my daughter's iPad. I spent my time there speaking with a number of residents and using the iPad to help them see places they had lived before, places they met the loves of their lives, playing them music they remembered etc. I remember the impact these conversations had with residents, how it made their day, as well as how powerful the iPad was for the residents to use and get involved with. It was by far the most gratifying and rewarding day I had been part of for some time.

It reminded me of the simplicity of kindness and the power technology has to help those who are digitally excluded. Digital poverty and digital exclusion are key challenges we all need to play a part in tackling as technology advances to ensure people are not left behind or forgotten about.

Dominic Hilleard
NED and Director of Executive Search

Avril - Love that, Dominic. Music has such an impact on our lives and brings back many fond memories. There is one song from Rage Against the Machine that never fails to bring out my inner headbanger. Ooh, and you thought I was a pop girl, eh? Na, none of those boy bands for me in my youth, unless they were called Metallica. Sorry Mr Barlow!

After a small headbang reminisce I'm keen to explore more. What initiatives are happening beyond the UK? I reached out again to Linda to ask her further questions, potato vodka cocktail still in hand.

What drove you to set up Energy Well?

Linda - I stumbled upon my business partner who had retained us to advise on a complex insurance claim on their power plant. We talked about the challenges of energy in Africa and how the Energy Well TM solution could address it. The term Energy Well TM is derived from the timeless tradition of villagers drawing water from local wells. We have taken this tradition, adapted it for energy and launched Energy Wells LLC, an energy supply company.

The motivation also stems from some personal experience. Whenever I travel to Africa I walk around like a weight lifter - in Girl Scout preparedness in case of a power outage. My handbag's extra weight is due to an overload of additional torches, chargers, candles etc.

Planning conference calls are anxiety inducing as limited power access means the line often disconnects. Pre-warnings of "excuse any typos, I am typing at full speed because there is a high probability of the network disconnecting" are frequent.

How does this link to the UN Sustainable goals?

The UN says: "We are committed to achieving sustainable development in its three dimensions – economic, social and environmental – in a balanced and integrated manner", via its Sustainable development goals: accessible and clean power, decent work and economic growth, industry, innovation and Infrastructure.

More than 600 million Africans live without electricity but yet more than 20 trillion cubic feet of natural gas remains undeveloped in sub-Saharan Africa. The Energy Well TM integration of these abundant natural gas deposits with modern renewable sources such as solar, wind and mini hydro schemes, plus state-of-the-art battery storage technology, ensures a practical and 'Africa-ready' solution can be provided. It will be managed with dedicated blockchain platforms that will provide immutable energy tracking and tracing and mobile money transactions.

Energy will be a key driver in Africa's industrialisation and active participation in the fourth industrial revolution. If the 2030 UN Sustainable development goals aren't achieved, it will not be due to an absence of innovation but due to DFI funding structures that are reluctant to provide development/seed/grant funding. It is objectionable to say Africa can't use its own gas under the guise of averting climate change when Africa is reported to contribute less than four per cent to the world's CO2 emissions, and the West industrialised on gas and other fossil fuels and refers to its use as 'energy security'.

• Natural gas can replace kerosene and wood burning, reducing deforestation, the high risk of fires and ingestion or respiratory deaths. As well as the burden on women and sometimes school age children who typically collect the firewood for cooking.

• The provision of affordable power will enable cold storage which is essential for food security. It will also support e-commerce to facilitate cross border trade with initiatives such as the Africa Continental Free Trade Agreement.

How will it scale?

An Energy Well can be scaled from micro energy supply from small to medium enterprises and domestic customers. It can be replicated at hundreds of sites within any region that has access to stranded gas supply.

What is your proudest achievement to date with Energy Well?

There is pride in having an edifying team and being an active participant in providing life-changing solutions to urgent real life problems:

(a) Connecting the unconnected via power and internet links has a large positive economic and social impact; improved access to health, education, employment, regional and international trade.

(b) Also proud of staying resolute that gas augmented by renewables was the way forward for energy security. Clearly exemplified by the Russia-Ukraine conflict, coupled with the nervousness around Energy security in UK and USA etc, and the way governments and business have galvanised to manage the geopolitics to ensure gas for power remains a core part of the power mix.

Linda Achan
Co-founder and CEO, NatureWrap UK and EnergyWells LLC

Avril - Linda, you amaze me every day – entrepreneur of two startups, both with a massive purpose and mission. I feel so warm and fuzzy. Up next, Tiffany also shares a wonderful story about connection.

Connecting the unconnected

Tiffany - We talk about the UK's digital divide with examples of a family all trying to do lockdown school lessons and homework on Mum's one mobile phone, or problems with very low bandwidth in rural areas. These are real issues for the UK, but one of my favourite tech innovation stories of all time is from 2007 when I heard about an internet server being driven around rural India in a bus, periodically stopping for villagers to connect over wi-fi to the server on the bus, usually from a single shared PC in the local shop. Then the bus would go off to a city to connect up, send the emails, load new web pages etc. The villagers would get reconnected next time the bus came through. Love it.

http://news.bbc.co.uk/1/hi/technology/6506193.stm

Tiffany Hall
IT industry professional, passionate about diversity
in technology and Tech for Good

Avril - Love it too Tiffany, creativity for inclusion.

We all have different lived experiences but how do we grow, learn and change? I asked Shereen Daniels, HR strategist, Chair of the African Diaspora Economic Inclusion Foundation, Managing Director of HR rewired, and someone I constantly learn from just that. Shereen very kindly allowed us to print an extract from her book, 'The Anti-Racist Organization: Dismantling Systemic Racism in the Workplace'.

Beyond the Lived Experience

Shereen - I have almost two decades of HR experience, working for a range of national and international companies, covering everything from risk management to books, fashion to food, telecoms to coffee. But it wasn't my HR experience on its own that got me here, and it certainly didn't happen overnight.

When I began recording a video a day for one hundred consecutive days, talking about my experiences but also offering words of advice, encouragement and challenge to decision- makers, I did not expect my soft-focus pixelated videos to gather momentum, but they did. Soon after, I was featured in Forbes, and became one of LinkedIn's Top Voices for 2020 and won HR Most Influential Thinker 2021 awarded by a top UK HR publication. Considering that I speak about racism pretty much every day, these are a few of it's one of the few social media 'trophies' I'm happy to display with pride. Then along with that came the comments. The emails. The voice notes. Phone calls, tweets and DMs. The tweets and the DMs.

From CEOs, founders, investors, diversity and inclusion leads, chief people officers and colleagues who realised their organization's had a problem. Or in some cases, problems, plural.

CEOs realised their companies were 'too white', and 'too homogeneous'.

The 'About Us' page on their websites suddenly became a focal point of conversation.

Diversity and inclusion leads quietly admitted that even under the banner of equity, their initiatives failed to specifically tackle race. Not in depth and certainly not in a way that gave them any confidence their workplace cultures were genuinely welcoming of all colleagues.

Chief people officers didn't know how to lead the change and were either pressured to do something, fast(!), or encouraged to do nothing 'and 'wait for the storm to pass'.

Investors responded to consumer pressure and public opinion and turned their focus to all white boards, citing governance risks due to a lack of diversity and social risks due to a failure to address social justice issues that have a material impact on people and communities.

Colleagues became vocal activists, collectively coming together across different ethnicities to not only to demand change, but to hold leadership teams accountable for 'walking the talk' and addressing racial discrimination and harassment that was the unchallenged elephant in the room.

A moment in time on 25 May 2020 had changed everything.

How is life different for your Black colleagues? What specific actions have you taken to dismantle systemic racism within your organization?

Or are you still mulling over what to do? Using euphemisms of diversity, equity and inclusion because specifically talking about race and racism still makes you uncomfortable?

The Anti-Racist Organization: Dismantling Systemic Racism in the Workplace is a book for leaders.

Particularly white leaders, who occupy the majority of executive positions in corporations on both sides of the Atlantic.

Those of you who:

• Suddenly have found yourselves having to speak with confidence and clarity about an issue that you may have avoided talking about – both personally and professionally.

• Want to exercise your power, privilege and influence to exact change for groups of colleagues, who to varying degrees, have been consistently silenced, marginalised and excluded from opportunities because of their ethnicity.

• Care about social justice and want to ensure that actions and interventions make a difference in a way that goes beyond ticking boxes. Who want to align anti-racism to their core values and their business objectives in a way that is meaningful and not performative or tokenistic.

• Have the ability to put your head above the parapet, to ask tough questions of yourself and others, and be prepared to listen, really listen and have your views, beliefs and perspectives of the world challenged.

• Are willing to work hard to resist feeling superior, of being the saviour, of taking action geared towards what looks good rather than what makes a difference and when times get tough, doesn't resort to "can't do right for doing wrong" thinking.

Shereen Daniels
HR strategist, Chair of the African Diaspora Economic Inclusion
Foundation and Managing Director of HR rewired
Extract from, 'The Anti-Racist Organization: Dismantling Systemic
Racism in the Workplace' (Wiley, 2022)

Avril - I fondly remember an amazing cup of tea with Shereen pre-pandemic. The sun was finally out so we headed to a table outside. Braving the elements for not even a quarter of the cuppa, we swiftly decided the wind was too much and speedily headed back inside, giggling and slightly shivering.

Reflecting on that moment, we throughout our lives make decisions and take certain paths. If you suddenly feel that cold chill of the wind on your path and realise you've made the wrong decision or action, it is in our gift to do something about it.

I wish I had more pages to share inspirational stories from the fabulous Dr Anne-Marie Imafidon MBE, CEO of Stemettes, a social enterprise encouraging girls and young women aged 5–25 to pursue careers in Science, Technology, Engineering and Maths. to the incredible Joanne Rewcastle who set up the Digital Voices programme at DWP Digital, because women are under-represented in the digital sector and we want more, visible role models to inspire others to find their voice and be a leader in digital. Judging the Women in IT Awards this year, there were amazing initiatives after amazing initiatives after amazing initiatives, all making a difference in this space. You know, I'm a big fan of Code Untapped founded by Ezechi Britton MBE and Jason Halstead.

As we head to some nuggets Eileen Jennings-Brown shared a brilliant quote I felt we must include:

"Most people ahead of their time tend to get overlooked in the present."

Wernher von Braun. Let's make sure that's not us.

Let's share wisdom!

"It is easy to say walk a mile in another person's shoes, but hard to do. We tend to think of ourselves in their shoes. If you want to build empathy you have to listen."

Michelle Spaul
Customer Experience Fan

"If you want to get picked for the team, you have to put your name on the sheet."

Sarah Lucas
Award winning IT Transformation and Change Leader

"It is not OK to be a knowledgeable egotist. No need to hide your expertise, but the way you share it says a lot."

Tracey Jessup
Chief Digital and Information Officer at the UK Parliament

"Leadership is entwined with the responsibility to be compassionate, kind, and accommodating."

Julia Smith
D&I writer, women's and LGBTQIA+ rights activist,
and a data-driven marketer

"There are two pieces of advice I have been given at various points of my career that have stuck with me:

The first is that acquisitions are guilty until proven innocent. I think this is a nice way of reminding us of the optimism bias we encounter when kicking off new things. The second is when I was promoted to Vice-President, my boss reminded me that that didn't mean I stopped having a role as a specialist contributor. I firmly believe that maintaining a strong connection to the detail of your teams' work makes you a better leader and manger."

Dr Alex Bazin
Technology Leader and Strategist

"Always keep yourself beyond your comfort zone. As soon as you are comfortable you stop growing."

Leon Gauhman
Chief Product & Strategy Officer at
Elsewhen. Angel investor and startup mentor
·

Avril - Before we move on, I know many reading do not consciously exclude, in fact we go out of our way to include and treat others how we'd like to be treated ourselves so how do we spot something we don't know we're doing? I called on a friend for help and asked for some advice.

"It's Inclusion for all, or it's not Inclusion at all"

Marsha Ramroop

Marsha - I feel this sums up what we're trying to achieve in the world. It echoes what many say about equality, for example, until we're all equal, none of us are, and about Covid, until we're all safe, none of us can be. It's what I strive for and won't achieve in my lifetime, but it is the work that I must do.

Quote from someone else:

"Years from now, our children and our grandchildren will look up and lock eyes with us. They will ask us where we were when the stakes were so high. They will ask us what it was like. I don't want us to just tell them how we felt. I want us to tell them what we did." – Kamala Harris, The Truths We Hold

This is all about action. It's not enough to just understand there's something wrong in the world, and to acknowledge it, or to be aware. We must do something, because future history is made now, by us.

I'd like to offer you Ten Top Tips to becoming more inclusive:

1) Start with Cultural Intelligence (CQ)

CQ is the capability to work and relate effectively with others. It's an introspective piece of work which asks, what is it about me that needs to change so I can be better at working and relating with you. And trust me, it's necessary introspection.

2) Ask yourself, who are my friends?

Have a look at all your messaging apps and contacts. Which groups are missing? Think about race, gender and disability, yes – but also think about geography, profession, socio-economic status. Address any gaps you find.

3) Confront your fear

Worrying about what will happen if you get it wrong can be paralysing when wanting to relate to those different from you. When you lean into that discomfort you learn and grow, a key characteristic of an inclusive person.

4) Listen, then listen some more

Those from discriminated-against groups need you to listen and believe them when they share their experiences. Don't deny them. Don't make excuses for other people's behaviour. Look at life from their perspective.

5) Accept and learn from mistakes

Mistakes are inevitable, it's part of being human. Just manage them differently. Listen, acknowledge, learn, reflect and move forward differently and your mistakes are more likely to be forgiven.

6) Accept tough feedback

Take feedback well, regardless of the spirit in which it is offered. There is always something to learn, even from the toughest moments. A truly inclusive person accepts feedback as a real opportunity to grow.

7) Accept you're biased

Professor Timothy Wilson says there are 11 million bits of information racing through your brain at any given moment, but you only have the conscious capacity to process 40. So much of your mental processing is unconscious and this shortcutting is the root of bias. You need to create procedural changes to mitigate its impact. Just knowing you're biased is not going to work.

8) Embrace diversity

Identify a group you find difficult to understand, discover common ground with an individual from the group and start to learn more about that attribute so you can grow and address any biases.

9) Check your assumptions

We jump to conclusions all the time. So, pause and think, "What assumptions might I be making here". Remember, whatever you think is true, the opposite may also be true. Explore lots of sources and check in with others with different lived experiences, for their opinion.

10) A list like this is just the beginning...

Becoming truly inclusive is like becoming physically fit; it takes time, effort, planning and constant practice. And you have to keep it up, otherwise you regress – but keep pushing yourself and you'll get to elite level, making it easier to upkeep. Take personal responsibility, only you can make yourself fitter.

Marsha Ramroop
One of the UK's leading CQ, cultural intelligence, experts

Avril - Thank you so much Marsha for the practical steps we can all take.

The best part about technology for me is that it is constantly changing, meaning we constantly learn and throw ourselves into new situations. OK, sometimes it would be nice to stay still, but where's the fun in that?

Chapter 8
Learn

Tick tock
Flick flock,
Tin turn,
Lean learn.
Avril Chester

Avril - The beauty of technology is the continual evolution but some days I feel like I'm in a parallel universe and the language is full of gobbledegook. Just when we think we got through to using plain English another acronym arrives. For example NFT – non-fungible token. Kevin, Anil, love what you are doing here, but a small plea for an easier name please. We all learn and remember things in different ways, what's your technique?

Dr Kuldip - In aviation simulators are used for several reasons – to train for normal operations as it is usually more cost effective and convenient than doing it in the real aircraft, but also crucially for non-normal operations such as defects, malfunctions and emergencies; things that we hope never to see in a normal day's work, but that we have to be able to recognise and respond to relatively quickly in a way that (hopefully) makes the situation better not worse!

We can of course learn about these things by reading a manual or a book, or in a classroom, or via Zoom, listening to experts explaining the cause of such situations, what to look for, what actions to take etc. The downside of these methods is that they are largely passive for the individuals being trained, and with the best will in the world, attention spans and the retention of such information can be less than ideal.

Real time simulation triggers and engages thought processes and responses in a way that cannot be replicated with passive training. The stimuli are visual, audible, sensory movement and produce accurate real time feedback on actions taken. For pilots, this trains them to recognise the signs and triggers of a developing situation and, crucially, reduce the 'startle' effect of something unexpected going wrong that can eat up valuable decision-making time in mentally processing what just happened!

Those familiar with the movie Sully: Miracle on the Hudson will recall the difference in outcome between knowing what's coming, when the FAA pilots in the simulators turned immediately for an airport after the bird strike (as they knew what was coming), and Sully being hit with something unexpected that no-one had ever trained for. In this movie the decision time was set at 35 seconds, which accounted for the 'human factor', or 'startle' effect.

Aviation safety is focussed on breaking the chain of errors, in other words, a series of smaller events, mistakes or omissions that can build into a larger and more difficult problem to deal with. We call it the 'Swiss cheese effect' – when something gets through holes in several defences. Unfortunately, accidents have happened because of a series of smaller situations building into something that became unmanageable within the time available for the crew to deal with it.

In business, the principles are the same. Admittedly occurring over a longer time frame and hopefully involving less fire, but in the same way larger problems in business can be created by the cumulative effect of smaller problems. Crucial in identifying these problems is recognising their signs and taking appropriate action early. Simulations are valuable in letting participants see the effect of these decisions in an interactive environment with a feedback loop, making those decisions and seeing them play out (or not, and if so, why not?) in a way that we can most easily learn from.

Equally, there is no guarantee in any field that the initial diagnosis of the problem or the actions taken will be fully correct in the first instance, this is why it's important to gather all the information realistically available within the time frame from a variety of sources to help make the decision, then once made, what is the outcome looking like? Is the situation improving? If not, have we missed something, is there another problem being masked?

In the flight deck we go back and continually review that the course of action is having the desired effect, making the situation better. In business it's the same, simulation provides the feedback loop on your actions, and review allows participants to fine tune or adjust their responses as the simulation progresses.

Simulation is the most valuable learning tool as it allows us to see, do, review, and learn until we see a successful outcome (or also seeing the series of steps which may lead to an unsuccessful outcome).

We have mentioned above the usefulness of simulators reducing the 'startle' effect on the flight deck buying valuable decision-making time. In business, exposure to scenarios in this way allows us to recognise triggers, and start to think: 'Ah, I've seen this happen before,' hopefully leading to a quicker decision-making process, and an earlier upward trajectory!

Simulation/gamification can be brought to your business and help you spot developing problems. Innovative Quality Solutions (IQS) have developed online simulations targeted at IT teams going through digital transformations to enhance the development process. The gamification platform is an educational approach to motivate cohorts to learn by using video game design and game elements in a learning environment. The goal is to maximise enjoyment and engagement through capturing the interest of learners and inspiring them to continue learning.

The facilitated digital simulation platform provides an experiential learning experience to understand the types of decisions you'll need to make at each stage of a three-year Digital / IT Transformation programme.

Dr Kuldip S Sandhu
CIO / IT Director & Management Consultant

Avril - Love it, Dr Kuldip. What a great idea to create a simulation for transformation. We also learn from our own adventures.

"This too shall pass."

Mark - A few years ago I found myself (pint in hand) in a discussion about running the London Marathon to raise money for the NSPCC, a charity that had come more into focus since becoming a parent. After another pint I had 'strapped in' and committed (along with couple of work colleagues who were also topped up with a bit of Dutch courage). A couple of quick nuggets from the whole experience.

Commit, declare, do. Running a marathon was certainly on my bucket list for as long as I can remember, but after the initial hook of raising some money for a good cause, declaring it to a few people I respect/care about who I knew would hold me to account really nailed it on.

Have a plan, but be agile. I had the standard training plan with the distances/times to aim for though NSPCC/Virgin and made a good start, but hit a wall after six or seven weeks when my training schedule fell apart after catching a nasty chest infection that I couldn't shift. I nearly pulled out as I couldn't bear the thought of not completing my goal.

After reassessing my options and with a few tweaks to my schedule I shortened my sprints and assessed progress every two weeks, setting new goals accordingly, eventually coming to the realisation that all I have to do is complete the course and it will be a personal best.

This too shall pass. This old saying has resonated with me most of my life but became particularly relevant when training – especially when it reminded me the burn in my chest and ache in my legs are only temporary and will soon be gone. With equal measures it helped me cherish the pleasure of finishing a run knowing I had really pushed myself while getting that little bit faster, fitter and stronger.

Mark Harrison
Seasoned Change Agent and
Technology Ambassador / Leader / Advisor

Avril - I'm in awe of anyone who runs a marathon, serious kudos to you Mark and everyone who runs. Your nugget, 'this too shall pass' applies to so many circumstances throughout life. So too does Daniel's advice: 'It's OK to say no sometimes.'

Daniel - When starting my career nearly 20 years ago as a spritely Quantity Surveyor, just 19 years old, never in my wildest dreams would I have imagined I would have ended up in the mind-blowing world of IT, surrounded by and dealing with some of the country's finest technological minds, and what a rollercoaster it's been so far.

While I still may be on my ascent, I sit here and reflect on the many learnings and experiences I've encountered along the way. Here are a few points I hope support others embarking on their own journey:

1. When starting any new venture, understand it will be anything other than plain sailing. Life is challenging and can sometimes even be cruel, but understand this – you are stronger and smarter than you know.

As the grey mist comes down, you may well indeed feel consumed but persist with it, fight through those times, and you WILL find a way.

Many a day I've looked up to the sky and wondered how we would find a way through, with bills mounting up and pressures building around, but in those times of adversity, persevere, dig deep, and know that this challenging moment is temporary, and tomorrow is a brand new day. The answer is always within you.

2. If you genuinely want to succeed in something, there can't be any half measures. You have to burn some bridges behind you to provide you with the path forward.

3. Don't go it alone. Find a supportive business partner, mentor, associate, or even a personal friend with whom you can share the rollercoaster. Ensure they can offer you balanced advice, encourage you

when things are going well, and provide honest feedback when maybe that's not the case. I have hugely benefited from having a business partner who possesses a very different skillset and knowledge to my own. This has helped address personal blind spots and provides a diversity of thought.

4. Learn to manage expectations effectively. A 'yes' person will always come unstuck. Be honest from the get-go, communicate constantly and openly, set goals, limits, and expectations. It's OK to say no sometimes.

Daniel Warburton
Co-Founder CIO Watercooler, where IT Leaders share ideas

Avril - What about technology? It is advancing and we're learning about it all the time? The world is full of scary stories, so thank you Beth for flipping the angle and writing about the positive steps we can make.

Beth - Technology is a tool that we can use to create, advance, and improve. There are huge benefits that come with using this tool. A quick Google search returns positive impacts as good news stories, like a drone helping to save the life of a 71-year-old man injured in a hard-to-reach area, a young woman creating algorithms to turn sign language to written word in real time, a paralysed man able to play a musical instrument for the first time using his eyes.

Like all tools, they can deliver both a positive and a negative impact, sometimes disruptive or abused through confusion, lack of appropriate training, or even through carelessness leading to errors.

A popular transportation company experienced a chilling example of this in 2016 when testing out some self-driving cars powered by onboard AI computers. One of the cars failed to recognise six red lights in a busy intersection with pedestrians present. It was originally claimed the incident was down to human error, however the media investigated further and found internal documents showing the error was due to the vehicle's mapping programme not recognising the traffic lights.

With self-driving cars just one of the ways technologies are set to revolutionise the transportation industry, this is a scary mistake and one that we need to learn from fast when putting decisions and control points into automated hands, especially as this is quickly evolving to equip technologies to learn from real life actions, making their own rules based on evidence-led situations.

This raises an important question – how do we make sure these tools make the positive impact intended? As a Process Lead, I see first-hand the way emerging technologies can improve business efficiency for my clients, their people, and customers. The most successful implementations are those that embed well with the people. In my experience this is through collaborative analysis, recognising ways of working and understanding the up- and down-stream impact. Having good representation of the people impacted along on the journey and strong governance framing the delivery of detailed, tested and well transitioned to-be designs is vital to any positive technology implementation.

Experience has taught us that technologies and their impact on people should always be at the forefront. Therefore, the recent roll-out of a system that ranks its citizens on their 'social credit' in China really grabbed my attention.

For context, people and/or companies are measured and then rewarded or punished on their everyday interactions. The system is currently voluntary, though the plan is for it to become mandatory and unified across the nation, with each person given their own unique code used to measure their 'social credit' score in real-time. For those who score poorly, this could mean they are unable to buy premium plane tickets or get good credit for mortgages.

It has been contended that this type of scheme would equalise the playing fields with privileges becoming available for those with good behaviour, rather than power and money. Alternatively, the extremity of constantly being watched is being heavily debated with concerns around privacy and automated decision making. Opinions between the scheme's participants themselves have also vastly differed. Some of those involved have fed back that it is a great initiative, making them become better people. Others are comparing it to a constant 'Big Brother' performance scheme, used to control and coerce good behaviour rather than steer it.

The proposed rollout of standardised and automated decision making, deciding real life consequences for people, drew similarities to an episode of a popular technology TV series, Black Mirror. Individuals were steered into good behaviours by being rated by peers following social interactions, leading to positive or negative societal consequences dependent on the rating. The Black Mirror series features multiple episodes showing how technology could continue to evolve and be applied within society. It is often debated whether the way an episode unfolds is down to the technology itself or the people's use of it and their responsive behaviours.

Like the above, some people promote the use of technology to deploy and decide positive or negative reinforcements on behaviour. Some of the more provocative episodes enact differing views on whether this is a dramatisation of a distant and far away dystopian future or more current and developing technology advancements. Concerning the latter, is it important to be objective on the potential impact of any advancement? How do we truly determine a positive impact, when outcomes can be viewed so very differently by individuals?

With AI poised to become a huge movement in the next five years and most major technology companies investing in AI technology right now, we should all be aware of the associated risks and lessons learned. The robot seems to make the perfect villain on the big screen and with robot-fear increasingly real, this area of advancement needs be better understood.

The fear of the unknown depicted in the dramatisation still appears to be very real with concerns around embedding bias into machines. This is valid and something that we should be talking about a lot more, particularly in conversations to align this type of decision-making technology to zero bias regulations, just as we do for ISO (Information security) certificates and GDPR (General Data Protection Regulation). If the AI seeds we are planting right now are to become our future decision makers, we need to ensure this is done fairly, through evidence-led policies and guidelines. Should we be giving unregulated decision-making abilities, and the consequences on people, to machines?

It is widely agreed that AI and emerging technologies can be used to create better and more efficient ways of working and living. A fitting example of this is the work being done in the SLR (Sign Language Recognition) space, with algorithms to translate hand movements to written words. The RNID, Working for Change Report found that 35% of business leaders surveyed in the YouGov poll did not feel confident about employing a person with hearing loss. Their Hidden Disadvantage Report found that 70% of people with hearing loss, who responded to the survey, said that hearing loss sometimes prevented them from fulfilling their potential at work. This is therefore a great positive stride in this space, and I look forward to seeing how the technology unfolds to help remove this barrier.

Continuing to push boundaries creates a real and positive opportunity to harness standardised decision making and machine learning and remove gender, race, age, social class, and disability bias. Over time this really could help to drive out discrimination and privilege in the workplace and other areas of our community.

It is the person behind any tool who shapes the motive for use and the form and range of the impact it yields. For example, a hammer can also be used to create, advance, and improve but can also be used to unsettle, control, and even hurt people when deployed incorrectly or misused. We should look at technology in the same way, having the ability to create momentous change, steer good behaviour and help people but also creating the ability to control and carry forward bias and bad behaviours from people to machine. This brings me to my final question; how do we ensure this does not happen?

The UK government recently conducted a review into bias in algorithmic decision making, setting out some key next steps for the government and regulators to support organisations to get their algorithms right, whilst ensuring the UK ecosystem is set up to support good ethical innovation.

A core theme of the report is that we can now adopt a more rigorous and proactive approach to identifying and mitigating bias in key areas of life, with clever use of data enabling organisations to shine a light on existing practices and identify what is driving bias. When changing processes that make life-affecting decisions about individuals it is advised to proceed with caution always. The report recognises the importance of realising that algorithms cannot do everything. There are some aspects of decision-making where human judgement, including the ability to be sensitive and flexible to the unique circumstances of an individual, will remain crucial.

Other key takeaways include the need for senior decision makers in organisations to engage with understanding the trade-offs inherent in introducing an algorithm. To be able to make informed decisions on how to balance risks and opportunities, they should expect and demand sufficient explanations of how an algorithm works, before deploying it in a decision-making process. Transparency is also key here in helping organisations build and maintain the wider public's trust in such implementations.

Findings contend that society will need to be engaged in this process. Technical expertise is required to navigate choices, however fundamental decisions about what is fair cannot be left to data scientists alone. Decisions should only become legitimate if society agrees and accepts them. Regulators and industry bodies should work together with technical experts and the wider society to agree best practice within their industry, establishing appropriate regulatory standards. The review recommends that there should be clear standards for anticipating and monitoring bias, for auditing algorithms and for addressing problems, encouraging the CDEI (Centre for Data, Ethics and Innovation) to play a key role in supporting organisations, regulators, and government in getting this right.

There is an ethical obligation to act wherever there is a risk that bias is causing harm and instead make fairer, better choices. Whilst embracing the positive impacts of technologies, it is also important to question whether this trajectory could change. It appears more work is needed in this area, with regulations welcomed to prevent/reduce any potential biases in this field, ensuring technology remains positive for all in the future.

Beth Younger
Process Lead at embracent

Avril - Brilliant Beth, such an important and great topic, there is an ethical obligation to act, how are you involved?

Someone I've met very recently who is extremely passionate in this space is Sherin Mathew (CEO and Founder of Innovation Exchange). Listening to and reading about his work, he makes me question where the ethical line sits.

Sherin is an AI ethicist and community leader, a former IBM AI Expert who decided to leave corporate life to create a difference with ethical innovations. He shared with me,

"While researching on how to apply AI ethics, I discovered a new human right – the human rights to Intelligence. It's to protect an individual's intellectual capabilities, such as job experiences, expertise, and awareness of our ecosystem; a human right that could save jobs from unethical AI innovations. I've shared a draft proposal of the new human rights and am currently leading a global campaign supported by international experts and collaborating with members of the IEEE, World Economic Forum, the UN – SDG, AI Council UK, DCMS, ICO and academics, challenging the capitalist approach by brands such as Google, Amazon, Facebook, Uber etc, who could commoditise intelligence before any AI regulations are in place. I predict that we will face 'Intellectual Colonisation' in a decade or two if this continues."

Want to learn more? Check out - https://publicintelligence.org/about/

"AI/ML with no ethics = ANIMAL."

Sherin Mathew
CEO, Founder, Activist, AI Strategist, Entrepreneur

Avril - We are learning and sharing all the time. Another pressing topic

is our home. Our planet and our climate.

Sean - The impacts of climate change are already being felt all over the world, including more extreme temperatures, threats to wildlife, loss of food sources, flooding, and lots more besides. In a recent report, the Intergovernmental Panel on Climate Change (IPCC) showed the difference between 1.5°C and 2°C of global warming. But unless we reduce emissions rapidly, the world is likely to exceed 2°C. By the end of this century, warming could potentially reach 4°C, possibly more.

Stats on pace of climate change

Average global temperatures have risen by more than 1°C since the 1850s. 2015, 2016, 2017, 2018, 2019 and 2020 were the hottest years ever recorded. The figures show us that the planet has been warming since the Industrial Revolution.

Sustainability has become an increasingly important element of a company's portfolio. Not only is it becoming mandatory for companies to report on their emissions and to start to create strategies to move towards net zero, and hence meet government committed targets, but it is also becoming increasingly important when it comes to doing business and attracting new employees to join your company.

They want to see evidence that you are taking sustainability seriously, and that it's not just a paper exercise, that in truth a lot of things are, when it comes to being compliant with specific standards. However, whilst it may indeed cause some additional outlay and in some cases will have a major impact, in addition to the obvious benefits to the planet, it will offer a business benefits such as:

- The opportunity to rethink your business model (which could well have been overdue anyway).
- The opportunity to save costs over time.
- The opportunity to take advantage of the latest technology available to increase your agility and speed to market.

Technology is not the only factor that will resolve our issues with climate change and enable all organisations to meet their net zero targets. However, it is ideally placed to play a major part.

For instance, moving out of costly, power hungry data centres to more carbon neutral environments provided by the major public cloud providers (hyperscalers), can immediately have a benefit. They all now offer tools to enable you to calculate your carbon footprint, when consuming the relevant services, which are all detailed below.

Microsoft (Azure) – https://www.microsoft.com/en-us/sustainability/emissions-impact-dashboard

Google (GCP) – https://cloud.google.com/carbon-footprint

AWS Customer Carbon Footprint Tool – https://aws.amazon.com/aws-cost-management/aws-customer-carbon-footprint-tool/

Some cloud providers are further ahead than others, but they are all moving in that direction, with the intention to go further. It is more difficult to obtain details on your carbon footprint at smaller public cloud providers, but there are free tools available that can help with this.

One such tool is the Open Source Cloud Carbon Calculator (sponsored by Thoughtworks) – https://www.cloudcarbonfootprint.org/

Used primarily with Azure, AWS and GCP, the solution is open and extensible with the potential to add other cloud providers, on-prem or co-located data centres.

However, we also need to be mindful that the carbon footprint of tech infrastructure now exceeds that of pre-Covid air travel, according to a report released earlier this year by French think tank The Shift Project, which says emissions generated by tech are growing at 6% a year. This is as a result of the increasing reliance on technology, whilst the corresponding improvements in efficiency are unable to keep up.

Edge Computing

Edge Computing is beginning to gain ground, with the advent of 5G. It is envisaged this will result in less power consumption. However, this is only possible if it can be deployed in highly efficient, AI-enabled HVAC (heating, ventilation and air conditioning) systems to handle the power and cooling of the servers. However, once you have many more distributed sites this becomes a more difficult expense to justify. This is particularly true when buildings haven't been designed and built specifically to be data centres but are instead refurbished buildings like the old central offices that many companies have. There are also security concerns regarding deployment and ongoing management of these. There are a series of measures that owners of these Edge Computing rooms can take to become more efficient, using the reduce, reuse and/or recycle methodology. These include:

Reduce
• Use renewable energy.
• Precise monitoring and liquid cooling / Switch off environmental units where possible.
• Power optimisation – cold aisle, warm aisle in your data centre.

Reuse
• Asset planning / Server life expansion.

- Waste heat recovery.
- Refurbished server rooms.

Recycle
- If you cannot measure – you cannot control.
- Recycle materials used in data centres.
- Ensure your provider has a roadmap towards net zero.

Virtual Desktop Infrastructure (VDI) is also being used to replace the need to have the latest and greatest laptops to meet the needs of developers and heavy users of resources, which also means that older, less capable laptops can be reprovisioned instead of being thrown away and replaced. In short, there are many innovative uses of technology already being employed, and these all need to be incorporated in your thoughts for your IT Strategy.

Guidance for Measuring and Reporting GHG emissions for Businesses

https://www.gov.uk/guidance/measuring-and-reporting-environmental-impacts-guidance-for-businesses

Greenhouse Gas Protocol and the Partnership for Carbon Accounting Financials (PCAF) methodologies.

PAS 2060:2014 Specification for the demonstration of carbon neutrality.

Finally, I just want to leave you with this. IT Leaders are ideally situated to enable their businesses to transition towards net zero and should take advantage of this opportunity to demonstrate their increasing value to an organisation. But you need to act fast, as the time window for getting this right is very short. And if not now, then when?

Sean Sadler
An IT Leader taking one day at a time

Avril - Couldn't agree more Sean, thank you for all the handy links and advice, hope you added plenty of arrow Post-it notes to those pages. It is important we really begin to understand the carbon impact of technology.

In a 2019 report published by The Shift Project (who I am a BIG fan of by the way), it was claimed online video streaming in 2018 was responsible for nearly 300 million tons of CO_2. This is 'equivalent to what a country the size of Spain releases in a year – for all sectors combined'. Let's get our heads round this for a minute, this was BEFORE Disney+ announced the launch of their streaming services and BEFORE lockdown. Shall I say the word BEFORE again. BEFORE.

As Sean also mentioned, 'tech infrastructure now exceeds that of pre-Covid air travel'. DW.com wrote about this comparing tech with the other industries we usually associate carbon emissions with, 'digital technologies have even surpassed the aerospace industry in terms of carbon emissions. While aviation's share of global CO_2 emissions is estimated to be around 2.5%, and rising, nearly 4% of all CO_2 emissions can now be attributed to global data transfer and the necessary infrastructure'.

Every time you upload or store that picture or video in the cloud you are contributing to the global transfer of data and necessary infrastructure. Do you really need to keep 25 copies of the same photo? Or all the previous drafts of your video creation?

Recent research from the Heart of the City suggests:

- A one hour video call between two people in London has the same emissions as travelling 10km by train.
- A one minute mobile to mobile call produces 57g of CO_2.

- An email of up to four words (like 'thank you very much') = 0.3g CO2e.
- An email with attachments = 50g CO2e.
- A one hour video call between two people = 290g CO2e.

I fear there is this myth that because we have reduced our work travel we are saving on our carbon footprint. Indeed, in some ways we are, but we are also simply transferring it to a hidden emission.

Whether you work for a technology firm, in a technology department or as the sole tech representative in a small organisation or startup, we are all keen to address our industry's growing carbon impact and learn together.

I wish to thank the Royal Institute of British Architects (RIBA) for hosting https://www.techcarbonimpact.com/ as part of their climate challenge activities. It is a wiki for all of us to contribute to. Please get involved and share your findings and advice. What are you doing? How are you influencing your supply chain? Have you added a paragraph to your job descriptions? I'm keen to learn from you.

Honestly, what I would love to learn or ask for is to agree on a standard calculation for tech consumption, then we know our starting point, comparing apples to apples, which will help us to target our energies towards the right solutions. There is a standard calculation for airlines, an average calculation for your flight so as a consumer you can act. What is it for tech? It'll never be perfect, but if we add number of devices, server room consumption, average data transfer and storage, cloud and cloud application usage etc, we should reach a decent informed place. But I bet if we all did this now for our organisations we'll calculate it differently. Some like Sean will use the open source cloud calculator, others will use something else. What are we all going to commit to and can we do it the same way, please?

Right, we know inspiration and learning sometimes come from the most unusual places. Time to channel your inner Buzz Lightyear.

Bitten by the Space Bug

Katherine - In early 2016, I needed a career move. My boss rang me up one day and said that the previous CEO of the UK Space Agency was leaving in a few weeks and they needed somebody to replace him – quickly.

I pointed out that I wasn't a rocket scientist (my predecessor was a rocket scientist) and I knew absolutely nothing about space. He assured me they had enough rocket scientists and that wasn't a requirement for the role.

I said I'd have to think it over.

I wasn't sure. It was a high profile position. I'd need to travel a lot in spite of having two-year-old twins, a five-year-old and an elderly dementia sufferer at home. And my mother in the US had just been diagnosed with an aggressive terminal illness. There was a LOT to consider and I wasn't confident I'd be up to the challenge.

I told my son about the call and that I wasn't sure I wanted to do it. He looked straight at me and said: "You know Mummy, if you don't try it, you'll never know if you like it. You should give it a go!"
So, then I had to walk the talk, didn't I?

Well, that was how I discovered my passion for space. I joined the UK Space Agency and spent the most stimulating year of my working life up to that point.

Yes, there was a lot of travelling and juggling. And yes, it was the year of Brexit with all the fall out from that, but it was also a year of many, many exciting space missions that my team and I managed to keep on track – in the face of change and uncertainty.

I was completely bitten by the space bug. The global space sector was changing so rapidly, I left government to start on a new career path – in space.

Most of us don't realise how much we take space and space technology for granted. The 1950/60s space race gave us: the laptop computer, cochlear implants, the Dustbuster (originally designed to collect samples on the moon), CO2 monitors, CAT Scans, memory foam mattresses – the list goes on and on – and satellites.

Today, we rely on satellites for everything from climate change monitoring to the time signal stock markets use to determine whether a trade happens a second before or a second after the market closes. Where would we be without SatNav in our cars and pockets, satellite TV, international mobile phone services, and, of course, the internet?

The pace of innovation in space is remarkable. The space sector is now full of entrepreneurial zeal and disruptive new technologies and business models.

While space is vast – it's also a unique environment and we have to take care not to destroy it. Early technologies left a lot of debris up there. Indeed, rockets were originally designed to get where they were going through a series of explosions!

Satellites that stop working become space junk. Collisions and disintegrating equipment create more debris. And a few nations (most recently, Russia) have flexed their military muscles by blowing up one of their own satellites – just to prove they can – creating massive clouds of debris that take decades to clear.

There are a million bits of space debris out there – both large and tiny – all hurtling around at high velocity. The world urgently needs to wake up to the increasingly harmful impact humans are having on the space environment before it's too late and we make space unusable for future generations! This is where I now focus most of my energies – working to keep space safe and sustainable.

This story started with me being uncertain about stepping up to a new challenge. Learning about space taught me to look up, stop focussing on the obstacles on the path in front of me and just be curious to discover what I could achieve and where the path might lead me.

As the late, great, Professor Stephen Hawking said:

"Look up at the stars
and not down at your feet.
Try to make sense of what you see,
and wonder about what makes
the universe exist.
Be curious."

Katherine Courtney
Mother, Strategic Advisor
and Chair Global Network on Sustainability in Space

Avril - OK hands up, who wanted to be an astronaut as a kid and what did we learn from running around the garden with a box on our heads?

Let's share
wisdom!

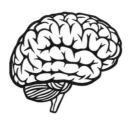

"Success doesn't come from perfection. It comes from learning: from mistakes, from others, from life."

Jane Deal
Mentor, Volunteer and IT Director

"The most inspirational leaders I have met in both business and sport have been totally humble as well as being great listeners. Spend five minutes listening to someone and only talk for one minute and you will start to find your own humility."

Peter Job
Founder and CEO of Three Tech Businesses

"Don't dwell on failures, learn from your mistakes, take on new challenges and most importantly focus forward!"

Dave Roberts
Award winning Tech Leader,
Global IT Director and Non-Executive Director

"Technology is an enabler for change not the panacea."

Dr Kuldip S Sandhu
CIO / IT Director & Management Consultant

"A much wiser person than I once told me that an aircraft carrier is a useful analogy for most organisations. As senior leaders, we imagine ourselves the pilots, immaculate faces beaming from the 'Leadership Team' page of our corporate websites, but in fact, we're groundcrew and as the leader of IT, we're the bottom of the ranks. We must support and serve our IT team so that they in turn can support the people in our organisation who actually serve the customers. Be humble and flip the org chart! You might think your ego will be bruised (it won't). Instead you will achieve better things, engender far more respect from your people; and get more done."

Peter Williamson
A lapsed quarry manager, experienced CIO and
charity trustee. Passionate about keep-it-simple
innovation and purpose-driven-business.

"The advice I wish I had been given as a new people leader – it is likely one of your team may need to talk to you about a personal issue, and it may be heart breaking. As a leader you cannot fix it and you should not try. You should listen and help arrange their work to allow them space and time to deal with the whatever life has thrown them."

Kelly Francis
I have an IT department in my head, and it's noisy in here

"The only thoughts and actions
you can control are your own. "

Craig Ambler
Independent Board Advisor and Digital Consultant

"However it makes you feel, it is always
temporary. Don't let the bad days define
you. Take action, take risks and enjoy the
ride. Learn from every day, trust your gut
and never give up. "

Laura Phillips
Loves solving problems using technology
and a huge dose of common sense

"To refer to the film Madagascar, 'just smile and wave.'"

Ian Wright
Chief Executive at Disruptive Innovators Network

Avril - I'm smiling Ian, I'm smiling. One of my favourite cartoon quotes I simply cannot help but sing is Dory's "just keep swimming" from Finding Nemo, and at Cancer Central we're doing just that. When I started my journey as an entrepreneur, I had all these grand plans. Some have seriously exceeded my expectations and others, well, talk about fizzle. I am relearning about company structures, finding new ways to deliver and relearning again. I've received more support than my wildest dreams. Thank you to every single one of you for buying this book. Collectively, I know we will find a simpler way to search.

Chapter 9
Search

I'm looking for something
You know what it's called,
But I can't find a thing
Even though I trawled.

Avril Chester

Avril - Finding trusted information easily, at pace, is vital in many circumstances but arguably it is most important when it comes to our health. This is the foundation as to why Cancer Central was created.

There's a lot of material about my story and why I started Cancer Central, so for fun, I asked my board to submit their stories for the book. Seriously, this is a great exercise, whenever you have an idea, ask your colleagues to relay it back to you, it's amazing what you learn. Of course, I'm awarding gold stars to each of my board members, I feel truly blessed to have their guidance and support.

You've donated as part of buying this book so what's Cancer Central all about? Take it away, Nigel.

"You are braver than you believe,
Stronger than you seem,
Smarter than you think, and,
Twice as beautiful as you'd ever imagined."

— A A Milne, Winnie-the-Pooh

Nigel - For me, everyone ever touched by cancer, whether as a cancer victim or a cancer survivor or quite simply someone who knows someone going through the challenges of cancer – this has always seemed a very apt message that would inspire us through the challenges of that journey to beat cancer.

When cancer first touched me it was in the form of my eldest son's other half. She was a wonderful, incredibly bright, beautiful person, both outside and in. She was also an aspiring doctor, challenging herself to follow her dad's pathway to a GP. She was destined for great things had her illness not curtailed that in the end.

But, when trying to support your son, members of our now collective families, and close friends through the journey that he and his girlfriend were on there's no personalised handbook to read or a hand to hold onto, outside of the specialist guidance given via our wonderful NHS. You suddenly realise there isn't ONE single information source or ONE single community of people that just knows how to guide you to all the right places for information about specific services, and key people you can talk to, to get help, advice and support.

It was all about accessing information, however and whenever I wanted and needed it, and in an easily digestible form. This was, for me, all about enabling myself so I could help others through the journey ahead. I found there was a driving force to connect and communicate with people who also knew what you and others around you are going through and WILL go through.

That's why when, over a coffee one day in London, I met a cancer survivor and inspirational leader called Avril Chester who told me all about her ambitions to build the ONE-STOP digital technology platform for cancer-impacted people, I knew there and then I had to find a way to help her and all the committed and dedicated volunteers to start and launch the company.

Cancer Central's mission is to help people in any way affected by cancer to find the support, services and information they need more quickly and more easily than ever before. People go through enough when touched by cancer, which is why our vision is to become the go-to place to find all the necessary cancer support, services, and information you'll ever need to access in the digital world we live in.

Everyone involved in Cancer Central is a volunteer. They give their time, skills, knowledge, experiences and energy freely. This, for me, truly makes this digital one stop shop for cancer support, an incredibly valuable gift for us all.

Nigel Hall
Portfolio Non-Executive Director and Chair of the Risk and Audit
Committee at Cancer Central

Avril - I remember that coffee very fondly, Nigel. Frighteningly more and more people are diagnosed with cancer every day, at all ages.

What's it like to be the parent of a young adult with cancer?

Alison - My eldest son had just finished his A-levels and was playing on the swings in the park with his girlfriend. As one of the nurses said later, it should have been the most enjoyable adventurous relaxed summer of his life before going to uni in the autumn.

But that was not to be. He jumped off the swing and felt a sharp continuous pain in his groin and testicle. This led to an immediate walk-in visit to the GP, which led to an emergency visit to A&E, which led to an overnight stay as the doctors weren't sure what was wrong. Best case scenario was it was nothing, worst case scenario was an infection. No one mentioned the possibility of cancer.

The next day an ultrasound scan led to the diagnosis of testicular cancer. My son went from a happy healthy young man on a sunny Thursday afternoon to a cancer diagnosis on Friday, less than 24 hours later. We were both in shock. He held on to the belief that it was an infection until the following week, when a CT scan and blood tests, and an emergency call from the consultant led to a confirmation of the diagnosis. On the Thursday afternoon we received the message: "I want to operate next week."

This resulted in our record week. Four hospital appointments at three different hospitals in five days, finally finishing on the Friday with an operation to remove his left testicle. He was offered the option of sperm banking. How do you discuss that as a parent with an 18-year-old? Who legally owns the sperm? How long do you want to store it? And can you wait on those grey chairs in a long white corridor before 'doing the business'? (I should add Mum went for a cup of tea in the cafe at this point!)

The NHS was wonderful and caring as always. How do you get a post operation 18-year-old to drink the standard offering of tea and toast? The answer: hot chocolate and ginger biscuits!

He had his operation and six weeks later went for chemotherapy. It's hard to watch your fit and healthy son become a former shadow of himself, like a deflated balloon. How do you say that you've deliberately taken him for a very short haircut, so if his hair does fall out it will be less noticeable?

There's a lot of information given to patients. We collected a pile of leaflets five centimetres thick – not that useful when he wouldn't answer his phone to unknown numbers for six months, and emails were ignored for nine months as he just couldn't cope. His mental health suffered as he'd moved from a happy carefree post A-level student to the dark world of a cancer diagnosis. No one tells you about the sitting awake with him at 3am as he reacts to the chemo; his mind, body and heart are in overdrive reacting to the drugs.

He's now a few years post-diagnosis and operation. He's got another few years of CT scans and blood test check-ups. Every summer he gets nervous as the annual check approaches. He's developed a fear of needles from all the tests. It's hard to catch a 6ft man when he faints.

That's why I'm committed to helping guide Cancer Central into the future and particularly the information search portal Ask Ave. Having a source of reliable, safe, clinically correct information in a searchable digital form is invaluable. No more five centimetres of leaflets and no more 3am questions about chemo that can't be answered. And of course my son lives in a digital world where Asking Ave is much more cool, private and personal than asking his mum.

My son is making great progress and is using his life experience to enhance the lives of others through supporting mental health in young men. He's living his best life. And I've changed my working focus to help Cancer Central move forward as the digital solution to disease information.

Every life experience moves you forward.

Alison McKinna
Portfolio Non-Executive Director. Finalist for Board Director of the
Year 2021, UK Women in IT Awards

Avril - 'He's living his best life'. As a small pause, I would encourage you to take every moment to live your best life. Give things a go, if it doesn't work, change and try something else. Sure, we all have regrets but consider this for a moment, I'm sure we have far many more beautiful memories than regrets. It's your choice which ones you choose to remember and make more of.

When I asked our amazing Non-Executive Directors if they were interested in joining Cancer Central's board, I cannot tell you the extravagant dance moves demonstrated in my kitchen when they said 'yes'. We met Professor Matthew Cooke through unexpected circumstances and I'm so thankful we did.

Prof. Matthew - I have spent my career as a doctor in the NHS. I am not an oncologist but working in emergency medicine, we see many people with cancer. For some, like Alison's son, they come to the emergency department not knowing they have cancer, for others it is the complications of their condition or their treatment, and for some it is the final stages of their life. But I am also a member of the public with family and friends who have been ill and had cancer.

I haven't had cancer, but about ten years ago had a diagnosis that could potentially mean that I could no longer work as a doctor and I may also have to change my life style considerably by not being allowed to drive and unable to be independent. I had so many questions to ask my consultant but tended to focus on the next treatment and the short term. In my consultations, I focussed more on my treatment than on how I would cope and adapt. I then went home and accessed information on the internet and from relevant charities. You could find out specific facts but it was difficult to ask broad questions. It was even more difficult to know who to trust in the anonymous world of the internet.

This made me reflect on my experience as a doctor. Had I offered appropriate advice? Had I signposted people to reliable sources of information? Had I focussed on medical care and rushed passed other issues important to my patients? Why was it so hard to get information about the things that mattered to me?

We all have different preferences on how we want to find information related to our health conditions. Some people prefer a face-to-face conversation, some prefer a webchat; others prefer to find information for themselves. Some want the personal conversation and to share emotions with a carer; others are more private. Some love the internet, others hate it.

Unfortunately, it is also a reality that most staff in the NHS do not have enough time to offer all the support they would like to. Hence, they often focus on the medical care. Patients also realise the pressure on clinicians' time and often don't ask. More often, the questions go out of our heads whilst we are in the consulting room and we only remember as we drive home. There are some questions that people don't know who to ask because they are not about their NHS care.

I first came across Cancer Central at the start of the pandemic. I was involved in a team looking at how people could access advice about this new virus and its rapidly changing treatment. Telephone advice lines were overrun with calls and many went unanswered. Cancer Central worked with others to rapidly create a 'chatbot' that could provide the latest information to large numbers of people via the phone or on the web. Whilst working with the team, I explored more about Cancer Central and realised that here was a source of safe reliable information for those whose lives are affected by cancer. It is easily searched using everyday questions and covers many of the important areas so often forgotten in a medical consultation. I saw a team keen to help people find information not only about their cancer and their treatment but also about living with that cancer, about surviving and about thriving despite the cancer.

Maureen Bisognano gave great advice to all clinicians – "Ask our patients, 'What matters to you?' rather than, 'What is the matter?'." For me, Cancer Central is part of providing that information about what matters.

Professor Matthew Cooke
PhD FRCEM FRCS(Ed) FRCP FFCI
Professor of Emergency Medicine

Avril - Thanks, Matthew. What matters to me? You'll frequently hear me say, I do not want Cancer Central to be built solely from my story. I wish for people who've been affected by cancer to have the opportunity to contribute. Whether it's an idea, an hour of your time, part of a project release, building the code, testing, writing policies, posting on our social media, designing our brand etc. We started life at a hackathon (which my mum cutely called Heffalump) back in April 2018. I wanted to ask the audience for ideas. I experienced the problem; I could see the need but how best do we deliver a solution?

Step forward our conversational search called Ask Ave; a chatbot to guide and bring relevant information to you. She was nearly called Avril but I wasn't going to talk to myself – I know some days I do and feel like I'm losing it – but not every day. Ave's been my nickname since, well, I can't remember. The 'e' has always been there too. No idea why, just pronounce it like the start of the word avenue.

I still feel some days Ask Ave is in diapers. There's so much content to learn in this space and we're exploring a new pivot with our content approach so please keep an eye on Cancer Central throughout this year as we implement our incremental learning and changes.

Back to Ask Ave, it was after a call from my Board Advisor Andrew Smith on the train home for first lockdown, where I was carrying endless bags and my box of Crunchy Nut, that I realised we could help even more. This story belongs to Mathew (yes, there are two Mathews on my board for the eagle-eyed amongst you – one has one t, the other has two). And yes, this is when Mathew and I met Matthew… there's definitely a tongue twister riddle in here somewhere.

Life is no dress rehearsal.

Mathew - I can't remember the first time I heard that. I'm sure it wasn't in drama at school, which I was terrible at by the way. I've always hated speaking to audiences and being in the limelight. I am happy in the background, the one manging the lights, the props, the music, and later in life I realised I enjoy being the facilitator, the networker, orchestrator, or architect. Especially when there is chaos and confusion around, this is when I am at my most visionary and creative. However, I'm a simple guy. It took me a while to really understand and appreciate the above statement. I will come back to it.

I have made mistakes, I still do. But I do not let them hold me back, far from it, I use them as an opportunity to continually learn and evolve and become a better person. Why did it go wrong? What did I or the team miss, how could have that gone better? How could I have improved the situation and/or outcome?

Ultimately what I have learnt is the older I get life has a funny habit of repeating itself, therefore those learnings will come in handy. After all, as Albert Einstein said: "Insanity is doing the same thing over and over and expecting different results."

In 2020, when the pandemic hit, I thought, OK this is new. It was a Tuesday evening in early March. As I sat watching a replay of the Prime Minister's earlier announcement about the impending lockdown, I received a call from Avril asking whether I thought the new Ask Ave AI chatbot design I was working on could help NHS Scotland and would I be interested in getting involved? She knew the answer was going to be yes before she'd even picked up the phone.

Within the next 24 hours those career learnings, the ability to reduce complexity and drive efficiency, were never going to be more crucial. I was finally going to be able to help make a difference and support our NHS. Our brilliant NHS saves lives, we all know that, but what most don't understand is that medical equipment is horrifically expensive; the investment in medical equipment and medical infrastructure to support the sick back to health. So, when we discuss legacy technology, we are talking about 10–20-year-old technology in some places, remember windows XP or 95!

The pandemic hit the UK in force and people wanted information; no, they demanded the latest information. They needed advice. There was panic and confusion. The advice was changing daily as researchers learnt more about the virus and how it spreads. The information age had never been more poignant and yet so full of misinformation.

To provide context, Scotland is made up of seven trusts and 110,000 care professionals supporting a population of seven million people. Up to date information was out of date before it could be cascaded out to the trusts, and over 100+ data points. Nurses, doctors, support staff were being stretched to new limits, because they still had to support all the other patient illnesses and NHS 111 was being overwhelmed.

After an initial briefing, I reached out to key global technology providers of our main platform and asked for their pro-bono support and licensing of their platforms that constituted my Ask Ave AI chatbot design, and support from our engineering partners to help integrate and support our platform until the NHS Digital team could support themselves.

The solution was designed as low code – minimal tech involvement to maintain once deployed. The idea being anyone with basic computer skills could manage and update the Ask Ave platform.

Initially, this was all new to the NHS staff and due to the historical internal complexity of their environments they queried the simplicity of it. I remember their shock when I shared, we would be fully functional and integrated within the week. "A week?" they said. "We weren't excepting an alpha version for at least a month or go live before six months."

Over the next month, they tested and tested. I worked with them through the internal boards and panels, provided them with answers, answered queries from key stakeholders, liaised with the national cyber security centre and managed relationships with our technology engineering partners. Within a month, still understandably being cautious, they went for a soft launch. This resulted in 40,000 enquiries from the public in the first 30 days. It blew us all away. With Ask Ave handling standard repeatable questions, such as: 'What are the symptoms', it began to free up vital resource on the 111 call lines for the more complex queries and concerns.

Two years on, Ask Ave is dealing with nearly a million queries and is a multi-award-winning platform. I sit here to write this as life returns to a 'new normal', where digital is fundamentally part of everyone's lives and smile. I look out of the window and hear the lovely sound of children playfully screaming as they are chased by their father in the park.

What is my golden nugget? There is nothing wrong with failing or getting it wrong. Always believe in yourself, be honest and truthful. No matter how painful, don't follow the crowd and try the unimaginable, for you will achieve greater things than you ever believed you could. Because one day, all that learning may enable you to make a difference you never dreamed of.

Life is no dress rehearsal. Make the most of your remarkable life, help others with no expectations or compromise, for you only get to play this show once.

Mathew Mallett
Chief Digital and Information Officer, UK Space Agency
and Chief Operating Officer Cancer Central

Avril - What a privilege we at Cancer Central were able to help in some small way, with big thanks to Mathew and our engineering partners Amido. As we emerge from our homes, for some travel is high on the list of things to do. I know it is for me and I may, sort of, well confession I did, book some holidays while locked in my home to explore places I thought I would never see. 2023 and 2024 are set to be epic in my world with once in a lifetime trips. The moral of that story is to never leave me alone dreaming. Are you thinking of travelling with or post-cancer? Check out Expedia's FAQ page.

Michael - Travel means many different things to people. It could be the holiday of a lifetime, a chance to experience a new culture, a time to connect with friends or family. Good times. But sometimes the thought of travel can make some people anxious for different reasons. This can sometimes be true for people who either have or had cancer. Many questions may be in those people's minds (or the minds of those who want to take a trip with someone affected by cancer). This can then become overwhelming and mean they put those worries aside and choose not to travel. So how could we help alleviate those concerns for people?

As part of Expedia Group's Day of Caring (whereby each employee can dedicate a day to giving back to the community) a group came together to create a FAQ page that helps arm people with answers to their most common questions when travelling with or post-cancer, with help from Cancer Central. The aim of the page was to use one of our existing page templates to really act as a central point for this information without it having any commercial element to it.

It's important people know they can use the page simply to answer their questions without feeling pressured to take the next step to booking their trip. I'm very proud of how we used our tech to create this for people and I hope it helps many to travel with confidence.

Michael Long
Michael has worked at Expedia Group for 16 years
and is passionate about both travel
and the inclusion of everyone in all situations.

Avril - Thank you, Michael and Expedia, for allowing us to be a part of creating this important page, travelling with and post-cancer - https://www.expedia.co.uk/lp/b/cancercentral-travel-faq_test?cache=false

It is incredible to look back at what we've achieved, and I get a little emotional thinking about it. You see, as Nigel mentioned earlier Cancer Central has been built purely through pro bono and donated hours in our spare time – a whopping 60,000 hours to date from over 250 individuals and 50 organisations. 60,000. I'm blinking as I'm typing. Please check out the 'Thank you' page on our website, we exist thanks to everyone involved.

I would also like to give a special shout out to our Advisory Panel; Simon, Andrew, Jon, Mark, Kali. The team: Tim, Steve, Niel and Liruss. Our Risk & Audit Committee; Jaspreet and Gillian. Plus The Data Company, ROQ and Amido who've given so much. Thanks for believing in me and Cancer Central.

We continue to have grand plans; we wish to grow, in particular grow sources of our content so that information returned is richer for those seeking it. Your donation from this book will help us to keep the site free of advertising and messaging charges and help us to continue to grow. You know, this book could make a good gift for someone (big smile). The best place to maximise your donation to Cancer Central is to purchase this book, or books (see what I cheekily did there with the plural) direct through www.nuggetstore.co.uk - thank you so, so much. Ooh and may I casually mention we have a donate button on our website (even bigger smile).

Will we become the go-to place to find cancer information and support? I hope so.

Will we work hard to achieve that vision and support as many people as we can along the way? I know so.

Chapter 10
Hope

Every day is a gift
Packed full of wish,
So go and explore
The future's all yours.

Avril Chester

Avril - Bring it on. There is no better way to end this book than to ask an absolute legend in the CIO community about the future. Grab your highlighter pens, you'll need them.

The Roaring tech-20s

Mark - On New Year's Day 2022, a tweet from the satirical (and often most accurate news summary) TV show Have I Got News for You? summed things up in just a few characters: "Unprecedented third attempt to restart 2020," it read. The dark humour captures the sentiment of two years of pandemic disruption. But within the joke, there is a scintilla of truth; we are at the beginning of the 2020s and there is a great deal to be positive and hopeful about, not least the role technology will play in making the 2020s an optimistic decade.

Technology has been instrumental throughout this challenging start to the decade in largely positive ways, keeping families connected, organisations in business, and will have been just one of the tools used by the researchers who have delivered a vaccine that has stemmed the impact of the virus. Through the coming years, technology will deliver precision, which in turn will enable us to deal with climate change and environmental degradation. A connected world has the power to distribute opportunity more widely, which will weaken dangerous polarisation. Although viewed with some trepidation, technology will continue to improve the ways we work, and the power of data can identify potential pitfalls and devise new ways to deal with the problems of organisations and society.

The Roaring 20s

When the initial impact of the pandemic began to ebb away, a number of brave souls said the world was about to enter the new Roaring 20s – historically referencing the 1920s, an era that is now famed for its arts, fashion and growth. The 1920s were also an era of incredible technical advancements. There are certainly parallels, and right here, right now, we can see the seeds of how technology can deliver some positive nuggets to our lives. Technology will be the roar of the 2020s.

Gartner, a technology business analysis services organisation, surveyed chief executive officers in 2021 and found the majority predict an economic boom throughout the rest of the 2020s, and that boom will be led by technology. Information technology will reshape and benefit society in six ways.

1: Precision

A remarkable amount of work takes place on the merit of the best guess. That is not to degrade the work, but at present, many of us lack the tools to precisely execute our roles. If the water system is leaking into the street, understandably, a team digs a hole where they can see the water escaping. Yet the leak could be a number of metres to the left or right of the visible escape; water will find the course of least resistance. Farmers will treat an entire crop; advertisers display to a wide audience. This 'spray and pray' approach has been necessary to date, but the 2020s will be the decade of precision.

Drones have gone from toys to moving sensors. Using the new 5G mobile telecoms network, they can fly over the top of entire almond tree crops and identify the exact tree with a fungus that will reduce the crop of that tree but, more worryingly, spread the fungus across the entire plantation. The high-powered heat-sensing cameras and connectivity (supported by new business models such as drones as a managed service) are able to scan solar panels and discover which panels are damaged and are not performing correctly. This allows the engineer to be precise in what panel they travel to and maintain.

The level of precision can be augmented as well. Suppose the visualisation captured by the drone is connected to an accurate database. In that case, engineers can analyse the inventory of that array and ensure they go to the maintenance job with the correct parts and tools. This reduces the downtime of the panel and makes the engineer's job more productive.

Large mines in Canada are already benefiting from this level of efficiency. Restricted to one-way systems for safety reasons, if a mine vehicle needs to return from the coalface, it can clock up a 17-kilometre journey, using fuel and increasing wear on the specialist vehicle. Drones are able to take items to the coalface, reducing the fuel bill.

Farmers cannot only treat a fungus with more accuracy; in a growing number of cases, our food producers can reduce their usage of chemicals. Precision delivered by drones, satellite imagery and applications that crunch weather and historical data provide insight on whether a chemical intervention is required or not. Chemicals are among the largest capital expenditure items in the growth of our daily bread. Cutting down chemical usage reduces the cost of food production, leads to healthier meals on our tables and, more importantly, positively impacts the natural environment. Agri-chemicals degrade soil quality, which reduces organisms and bug life and breaks the natural world's lifecycle. A bottle of fungicide is the first step in the reduction of wild birds in our skies; if we farm more precisely, we get more songbirds.

If drones are moving sensors, static sensors also allow for a more precise environment. As we will discover, technology is creating a more distributed world, which means buildings that in 2019 were constantly occupied – think offices, shops, conference centres and transport buildings – will now be as necessary as before, but not used to the same levels. The management of the built environment will become sensor analysed and connected.

Local government bodies are already at the forefront of this. Their buildings are vital to communities, but usage levels have been changing over several decades. Periods of low use can waste energy on lighting, cooling, or heating. Turning utilities off allows dampness to build up, so maintenance has to be done, but with sensors in place, Norfolk County Council has improved the management of its estate, ensuring utilities are used to protect the buildings efficiently and deliver services to the residents.

2: Connected and Distributed

Technology enabled employees to work at home through the dark days that opened the 2020s, and this kept organisations operating. For many, not all, the ability to work flexibly has been a boon. We have a golden opportunity to allow technology-oriented work to become highly distributed. In the last decade, London and Manchester dominated the national economy, wonderful cities as they both are; their strength was to the detriment of the nation's other cities, towns and villages. A digital economy should be able to thrive as well on the Downs as it does in the city. Digital workers can enable local communities to bounce back as they no longer only see their community after work but are able to blend local and city centre working and living more easily.

Rebuilding the economy for a better 2020s will require rewiring. Connecting up the towns and villages so that, if workers chose to, every kitchen, spare bedroom or even shed could be part of the digital economy, whether nestled in a remote valley, facing the sea or atop a global headquarters in Canary Wharf.

The opportunity is about more than using technology. If technology-oriented jobs are distributed beyond the powerhouse cities for at least part of the week, this will be a tide that raises all ships. More active work in every corner of the nation can provide further work to those in our communities. If footfall to the rural station, the local cafe/pub and barbers improves, then opportunity of all kinds spreads. The challenge is for all members of a community to embrace this opportunity, not to preserve our towns and villages in some form of outdated conservatism, but to re-imagine rural life and cities as a blend of the modern digital economy as well as retaining roots to the history that first created those conurbations.

That same connectivity will go beyond our own island too, and that is to be welcomed, as by sharing the connectivity opportunity we can share and deal with global challenges.

3: Automatic for the people

Automation and robots have appeared in negative headlines, but if harnessed correctly, automation can be highly beneficial for society. Every job has elements of routine and burdensome necessity. In the worst cases, the routine becomes the sole purpose of a role. Yet technology like robotic process automation (RPA) can remove those routine tasks and free people's minds from following linear processes every month-end or quarter and allow their brains to wander free and create ideas and opportunities.

In healthcare, this is ensuring that good levels of information gathering are retained for governance purposes but freeing clinical staff up to care for patients. Successful deployments of automation technology like RPA describe the bot as an additional team member supporting staff. In an age of skills shortages, allowing team members to develop and not spend their working days on routine is a valuable development and one that will grow and grow over the 2020s.

Automation in the form of autonomous machines is equally feared; however, this is the course of history, and again, if well managed, can be beneficial. The factory line and the harvester have removed a wide number of jobs from the employment market, but in their place, we needed more highly skilled maintenance crews, planners, engineers, and an entirely new supply chain both to feed raw materials into the machines, but also to distribute the goods that are the outcome of automation. The infrastructure that exists today is not fit for a more autonomous society. One of the most exciting opportunities society faces is to develop new infrastructure that supports active living for people and enables autonomous robots to travel alongside self-driving vehicles.

The adoption of autonomous ways of working is already taking place. A technology leader at a major NHS trust, for example, talks of nurses and clinicians entering healthcare that have little experience of pen and paper. These carers will be used to a level of automatic digital service from their personal lives and possibly education; they will therefore expect autonomous support in their roles, so they can do what they want to do – care and cure.

And no discussion about automation can exclude artificial intelligence, again a technology that stokes up levels of fear. There are concerns, but the data levels already produced by society and the rising levels of data that a digital society will create demand a technology that can ethically manage the data. Once again, healthcare is leading the way with cancer and eye clinical uses of AI proving beneficial to carer and patient alike.

4: Data identifies the opportunities

For society to become precisional, connected and for the drudgery to be automated, there will be a reliance on data. Until recently, data has been created largely for the sake of collecting and creating data. However, the opportunity of the 2020s is to use data to fill the gaps in knowledge, to identify where to be more precise and how to automate.

Already water authorities are using sound data to monitor the clean and waste water systems we all rely on and prevent a blockage. This leads to predictive maintenance and cleaner water. The terrible Genoa bridge failure in Italy that led to the loss of 43 lives is unlikely to be repeated; the bridge that replaced it has sensors and data dashboards monitoring the traffic and every element of the structure, again allowing predictive maintenance.

All of this data is enabling the development of digital twins. Anybody who has tried to plan a room will appreciate how difficult it is to imagine the physical world when it either does not exist or is inaccessible. Digital twins allow organisations to get close proximity to the physical world and carry out experiments safe in the knowledge that digital is, essentially, not real. Engineering, architecture, healthcare, and many unimagined scenarios can be rehearsed.

5: Shared planet responsibility

Describing the 1920s as roaring ignores what was to follow. The 1930s were beset with nationalism that led to the Holocaust and a world war. Technology has been powerful and positive, but technology-oriented organisations have also fed the imbalance in our society, with tech firms exploiting low paid workers, enabling disinformation about immigration, faiths, nations and most alarmingly, the pandemic. This has already led to division across society.

During the pandemic, the digital divide in society was clearly seen. Remote online schooling only works if teachers and pupils have access to the right types of tools to educate and learn. A classroom is no more than a room if there are no books, desks and whiteboards, and the technology industry needs to ensure that education providers and pupils have access to the right tools. Citizens must play their part, too, a smartphone is powerful but not always the best tool for understanding science lectures or composing an essay.

Technology is both part of the answer to climate change and part of the problem. Dirty and inefficient data centre providers are not really the answer to reducing corporate flights. The technology sector and technology users must ensure that increased connectivity and computer power do not exacerbate the extreme weather and melting of the polar ice caps. As an industry, technology has enormous potential to move to a circular economic model, with greater re-use of the materials it uses to connect, collect and analyse all our data. Dealing with climate change will rely on technology. The scale of the challenge is such that the power of AI, cloud computing, automation and sensors will be necessary to keep carbon levels in check and to enable opportunity without the planet paying the price.

6: Next generation technology

Following the recent rebranding of Facebook to Meta, there has been a great deal of talk about the metaverse and the next generation of technologies. Following the Meta rebrand, Microsoft's acquisitions in the gaming sector were, as its CEO revealed to the Financial Times, about more than first-person shooter games. Microsoft sees the metaverse as having huge potential in business and, therefore, to non-gaming services. Consumers are already beginning to spend time in the metaverse, for instance on exercise platforms like Zwift or Nordic Track, the digital twin technology mentioned above is coming to retail, healthcare and the automotive sector.

Given the pace of change that the 2000s have witnessed and the level of technology adoption that took place during the pandemic, it would be unwise to bet against the metaverse.

Many technologies have initial periods of early adoption and find real use cases at a later date – often once the hype has died down, drones are a classic example.

The Roaring tech-20s

The 2020s will be roaring. That roar will come from technology, but it is important to learn the lessons from the last Roaring 20s. The 1920s left many behind, as wealth congregated in certain pockets of society and trailblazing industries. This created a divide in society that was all too easily exploited.

Suppose technology is to be the fabric of our society. In that case, it is vital that technology takes responsibility for those in society that are vulnerable, for being an active and credible member of communities where business takes place, and for ensuring that as it grows as an industry, it reduces its impact on the planet. Technology will continue to improve the ways we work, and the power of data can identify potential pitfalls and devise new ways to deal with the problems of organisations and society. Developed with care and responsibility, technology will deliver a roaring 20s.

Mark Chillingworth
European business writer specialising in technology leadership and
chair of the Horizon CIO Network

Let's share
wisdom!

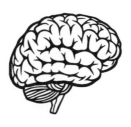

"Confidence opens doors.
Courage opens possibilities. "

Catherine Ann Reid
CEO Doqit. Passionate about making a positive contribution to
the wellbeing of people and the planet

"Sustainability is key. In your career
and in life, you are here to leave a
legacy. Tread carefully, build and plant
the seeds to grow, so that all those you
meet can stand on their own. "

Kim Fitzpatrick
Award winning Technology Director and Leader,
passionate about sustainability

"It's important to share the kindness in business and giving time is the greatest gift you can give another entrepreneur."

Victoria Russell
Business Coach and Angel Investor

"We need strength while doing the possible, but we need faith while doing the impossible."

Aju Alexander
A Passionate Technologist and Serial Entrepreneur

"Always be true to yourself; only then can you really step into your power!"

Cheryl Cole
Editor DiversityQ

"Overcoming challenges is part of life. When we do this with compassion, humour, humility, rather than power and force, the world is a better place."

Alison McKinna
Portfolio Non Exec Director including to Cancer Central. Finalist for
Board Director of the Year 2021, UK Women in IT Awards

"It's OK to start over – in life, love, career, anything! Whatever age you are, start over as many times as you need to."

Fran Grant
An Executive Search Consultant, recruiting Senior Technology and Digital Leadership positions. She is also a mum to three young boys and a published author of five books

Avril - This is life.

Go invent, eat, give others a boost, thrive in change, include, learn, search and live in hope. To quote Mark Chillingworth, "technology will deliver a roaring 20s", I'm super excited to be a part of it, are you?

"Nothing we do can change the past, but everything we do changes the future."

Ashleigh Brilliant.

What is your future?

Boom (& mic drop)
'Tech Treats & Treasures'
By Avril Chester

Cancer
Central

Enjoyed this book?
Order one for a friend from
www.nuggetstore.co.uk
and help raise more money for
Cancer Central

What is your One Golden Nugget?
www.onegoldennugget.com